In the Flames of Discord: Exploring the Israeli-Hamas Conflict in the Gaza Strip

Comprehensive study of the roots, causes and global impacts of an intricate contemporary conflict, enriched by reflections on the value of human tolerance during periods of crisis.

Modern Wars

1. Historical context of the region: from the creation of the State of Israel to the current conflict.

2. Origins and ideology of Hamas.

3. Immediate cause of the current conflict.

4. Military strategies and tactics used by both sides.

5. Effects of the conflict on the civilian population.

6. Reactions of the international community to the conflict.

7. The role of media and propaganda in shaping perceptions of conflict.

8. Attempts at mediation and peace negotiations.

9. Economic impact of the conflict on Gaza and Israel.

10. Personal experiences of those living in the midst of conflict.

11. Long-term effects of the conflict on the region.

12. Perspectives for a peaceful and sustainable solution.

13. Role of international organizations in conflict management.

14. Reactions of the Palestinian and Israeli diaspora to the conflict.

15. Analysis of previous treaties and agreements that have influenced the current situation.

16. Role of the United States and other world powers in the conflict.

17. Possible regional implications of the conflict.

18. Stories of refugees and those displaced by the conflict.

19. Role of natural and territorial resources in perpetuating conflict.

20. Personal reflections on humanity and tolerance in situations of conflict.

The historical context of the region is crucial for understanding the conflict between Israel and Hamas in Gaza. Here are a few key points that might be included:

1.1 The creation of the State of Israel in 1948 and the war of independence: After Israel's declaration of independence in 1948, a war broke out between Israeli forces and neighboring Arab countries, including Egypt and Jordan. This war led to the creation of the State of Israel and the flow of hundreds of thousands of Palestinian refugees.

1.2 Occupation of the West Bank and the Gaza Strip: After the 1967 war, Israel occupied the West Bank, East Jerusalem and the Gaza Strip, creating growing tensions with the Palestinian population living in these areas.

1.3 Oslo Intifada and Negotiations: In the
80s and 90s, two Palestinian intifades took
place against the Israeli occupation,
leading to peace negotiations between
Israel and Palestinian leaders, culminating
in the Oslo accords in 1993.

1.4 Unilateral withdrawal from Gaza: In
2005, Israel evacuated all settlements and
military forces from the Gaza Strip, ending
direct occupation. However, it maintained
substantial control over borders and access
to the Gaza Strip.

1.5 Rise of Hamas: Hamas, a Palestinian
Islamic group, has gained political and
military power in the Gaza Strip,
challenging the authority of the Palestinian
Authority and giving rise to tensions with
Israel.
These are just a few of the pivotal moments
in the region's history that have helped
shape the current conflict between Israel
and Hamas in Gaza. It is important to
carefully examine how these events have

influenced political, social and economic dynamics in the region and have contributed to the current situation.

1.6 Subsequent Arab-Israeli Wars: After 1948, the region saw a series of armed conflicts between Israel and its Arab neighbors, including the 1956 war and the 1973 war (also known as the Kippur War). These conflicts have helped to strengthen divisions and tensions in the region, further complicating peace efforts.

1.7 Colonization and settlement in the West Bank and East Jerusalem: After 1967, Israel began building Jewish settlements in occupied Palestinian territories, creating tensions with the local population and questioning the feasibility of a two-state solution.

1.8 Camp David and Oslo peace accords: In 1978, the Camp David peace accords brought peace between Israel and Egypt. The 1993 Oslo accords and the negotiations that followed created the basis for Palestinian authority and partial Palestinian autonomy in the West Bank and Gaza.

1.9 Settlement expansion and the separation wall: Despite efforts for peace, Israel has continued to expand settlements in the West Bank and to build the separation wall, contested by the international community as a violation of international law and an obstacle to peace.

1.10 Second Intifada: In 2000, the Second Intifada broke out, a Palestinian uprising against the Israeli occupation, characterized by widespread violence and terrorist attacks. This period of violence has further damaged trust between the two sides and has made it more difficult to reach a negotiated solution.

1.11 Hamas elections and the blockade of Gaza: In 2006, Hamas won the Palestinian legislative elections, leading to an escalation of tensions with Israel and the imposition of a blockade on Gaza, which had serious humanitarian consequences on the civilian population.

1.12 Conflicts in Gaza: Over the years, several armed conflicts have occurred between Israel and Hamas in Gaza, including Operation Cast Lead in 2008-2009, Operation New Arc Column in 2012, and Operation Protective Edge in 2014. These conflicts have caused serious infrastructure and humanitarian damage and have helped to reinforce the cycle of violence in the region.

These are just a few of the significant events and developments in the history of the region that have influenced the conflict between Israel and Hamas in Gaza. Understanding this historical context is crucial for analyzing the complex dynamics and root causes of the conflict.

1.13 The issue of Palestinian refugees: After the creation of the State of Israel in 1948, hundreds of thousands of Palestinians were forced to flee or were expelled from their homes, becoming refugees in other Arab countries or within Palestine itself. This refugee issue has remained unresolved and is one of the most divisive issues in peace negotiations.

1.14 The religious dimensions of the conflict: The region is sacred to Jews, Muslims and Christians, with important religious sites for all three religions. The dispute over holy places such as the Esplanade of Mosques for Muslims and the Western Wall for Jews has added a religious dimension to the conflict.

1.15 Palestinian internal divisions: The political and ideological divisions between Palestinian factions, in particular between Hamas and Fatah, have complicated efforts for a unified leadership and a common strategy in the fight against the Israeli occupation.

1.16 The role of regional actors: Countries such as Iran, Saudi Arabia and Turkey have influenced the conflict through political, financial and military support for various Palestinian factions or Israel, further complicating the regional framework.

1.17 The construction of the separation wall: Israel built a separation wall in the West Bank to protect itself from terrorist attacks, but this created physical divisions and caused discomfort for many Palestinian communities, fueling tensions.

1.18 Diplomatic efforts for peace: Despite the challenges, there have been numerous international efforts to resolve the Israeli-Palestinian conflict, including peace negotiations, international conferences and mediation initiatives, however, so far none of these efforts have led to a lasting solution.

1.19 The humanitarian situation in Gaza: Due to the blockade imposed by Israel and internal political instability, the Gaza Strip faces serious humanitarian problems, including shortages of food, water and medical care, as well as widespread unemployment and extremely difficult living conditions for the civilian population.

1.20 Daily violence and constant tensions: Daily life for the inhabitants of the region is marked by violence, military incursions, terrorist attacks and reprisals, fueling a climate of fear, suspicion and resentment that makes it difficult for both sides to find a way out of the conflict.

1.21 Relations with the international community: The Israeli-Palestinian conflict has attracted the attention of the international community since its origin. The United States has historically been a strong ally of Israel, while many European and Arab countries have supported the

Palestinian cause. International organizations such as the UN have played an important role in trying to resolve the conflict, but they have often encountered political and diplomatic obstacles in trying to enforce resolutions and promote lasting peace.

1.22 The issue of contested borders and territories: One of the crucial points of contention in the conflict is the issue of contested borders and territories, in particular the West Bank and East Jerusalem. Both sides claim these territories as an integral part of their state, making it difficult to reach an agreement on the borders and the status of these areas in peace negotiations.

1.23 The role of non-violent movements and civil resistance: Alongside armed resistance, there have also been non-violent and civil resistance movements on both the Israeli and Palestinian sides. These include peaceful protests, hunger strikes, and actions of civil disobedience, which have tried to draw attention to the situation and promote a peaceful solution to the conflict.

1.24 The psychological consequences of the conflict: Violence and chronic instability have had serious psychological consequences on both the Israeli and Palestinian populations. Many people, especially children, have experienced trauma and post-traumatic stress due to exposure to violence and the loss of family and friends.

1.25 Reconstruction and development efforts: After each cycle of violence, there have been efforts to rebuild damaged infrastructure and to promote economic and social development in the affected areas. However, the cycle of destruction and reconstruction continues to perpetuate a vicious cycle of poverty and instability.

1.26 The role of the media in the conflict: The media, both local and international, have played a significant role in shaping perceptions and narratives of the conflict. The use of images and narratives that are often partial or biased has helped fuel the conflict and influence international public opinion.

1.27 The prospects for a peaceful solution: Despite challenges and divisions, there are still hopes and efforts for a peaceful solution to the conflict. These include the search for a political agreement based on coexistence and mutual respect, as well as a commitment to dialogue and mutual understanding between the two communities.

1.28 The importance of education and awareness-raising: Education and awareness-raising are essential to promote understanding and tolerance between Israelis and Palestinians. Investing in education and the promotion of the values of peace and coexistence can help create the basis for a future generation of leaders and citizens committed to peace and justice.

1.29 The issue of prisoners: The issue of prisoners is a sensitive issue in the Israeli-Palestinian conflict. Both sides have been holding political and military prisoners, causing tensions and negotiations for their release. The conditions of detention and the treatment of prisoners have become topics of debate and criticism by human rights organizations.

1.30 The impact of the diaspora: The Palestinian and Israeli diaspora played a significant role in the conflict, both as supporters of the Palestinian cause and as supporters of Israel. The Palestinian and Israeli communities abroad have tried to influence international public opinion and to play a role in peace negotiations, bringing different and often conflicting perspectives.

1.31 The role of natural resources: The control of natural resources, in particular water, has fueled tensions in the conflict. The dispute over water resources in the region has helped to aggravate divisions and complicate efforts for a negotiated solution.

1.32 The importance of leadership: Leadership has been critical in determining the course of the conflict and peace efforts. The actions and decisions of political and military leaders have had a significant impact on the dynamics of the conflict and on the prospects for a peaceful resolution.

1.33 The use of technology in the conflict: Technology has played an increasingly important role in the Israeli-Palestinian conflict, with both sides using advanced weapons, drones, cyber warfare and other technologies to conduct military operations and intelligence. However, the technology has also been used for civilian purposes, such as communication and political mobilization.

1.34 Political and social polarization: The conflict has contributed to increasing political and social polarization both in Israel and in the Palestinian territories. Internal divisions and differences of opinion over conflict management have made it difficult for both sides to find common ground and work together for a peaceful solution.

1.35 The importance of justice and reconciliation: Justice and reconciliation are fundamental to addressing past injustices and building lasting peace. Working for truth, justice and forgiveness can help overcome divisions and build a more stable and inclusive future for all the inhabitants of the region.

1.36 The role of religion in the conflict: Religion has played a complex role in the conflict, both as a source of inspiration and motivation for both sides, and as an element of division and conflict. Understanding the religious dimensions of the conflict is essential to address its deep roots and to promote dialogue and mutual understanding.

1.37 Civil society engagement: Civil society plays a crucial role in promoting peace and human rights in the region. Non-governmental organizations, activists, artists and other members of civil society have worked to raise public awareness, promote intercultural dialogue and support peace and reconciliation initiatives.

1.38 The issue of refugees and displaced persons: The conflict has caused the creation of a large population of refugees and displaced persons, both Palestinians and Israelis. The issue of refugees has become one of the most controversial and divisive issues in the conflict, with many families fighting for the right to return to their homes and homelands.

1.39 The impact of terrorism and extremism: Terrorism and extremism have played a significant role in the conflict, with radical groups carrying out attacks against civilians and infrastructure both in Israel and in the Palestinian territories. The fight against terrorism and extremism represents a key challenge for both sides in pursuing lasting peace and security in the region.

1.40 The complexity of regional relations: The Israeli-Palestinian conflict takes place in a complex regional context, characterized by interstate conflicts, geopolitical rivalries and diverging interests. Relations with countries such as Iran, Turkey, Saudi Arabia and other regional actors have influenced the conflict and the dynamics of the Middle East as a whole.

1.41 The issue of UN resolutions: Over the years, the General Assembly and the United Nations Security Council have adopted numerous resolutions concerning the Israeli-Palestinian conflict. These resolutions addressed various issues, including the Israeli withdrawal from the occupied territories, the recognition of the rights of Palestinian refugees, and the achievement of a negotiated two-state solution. However, many of these resolutions have not been fully implemented, and the Security Council has often been paralyzed by a lack of consensus among its permanent members.

1.42 The challenge of disinformation and propaganda: In the Israeli-Palestinian conflict, both sides engaged in disinformation and propaganda activities to influence national and international public opinion. This includes the dissemination of distorted narratives, the manipulation of images, and the use of emotional rhetoric to justify military actions and demonize the adversary. The spread of disinformation has further complicated the search for a peaceful solution to the conflict, creating divisions and fueling hatred and mutual mistrust between the two communities.

1.43 The role of international organizations and civil society: International organizations such as Amnesty International, Human Rights Watch and Oxfam have played an important role in monitoring and documenting human rights violations in the Israeli-Palestinian conflict. These organizations have provided humanitarian assistance, supported the rights of refugees and vulnerable populations, and sought to promote a peaceful, human rights-based solution to the conflict. Likewise, civil society, including activists, academics, artists and grassroots groups, has played a crucial role in promoting peace, human rights and social justice in the region through awareness-raising, advocacy and popular mobilization initiatives.

1.44 The question of human rights and international law: The Israeli-Palestinian conflict raises important issues related to human rights and international law. Human rights violations, including arbitrary killings, arbitrary detentions, house demolitions and land confiscations, have been documented by numerous human rights organizations and condemned by the international community. Likewise, the Israeli military occupation of the occupied Palestinian territories has been considered illegal by the majority of the international community and has aroused criticism for its duration and impunity.

1.45 The importance of dialogue and reconciliation: Dialogue and reconciliation are fundamental to overcoming divisions and building lasting and inclusive peace in the region. This requires a sincere commitment on both sides to overcoming differences and working together to address past injustices, promote mutual understanding, and build a foundation of trust and mutual respect. Initiatives of dialogue and reconciliation, including community meetings, shared educational programs and economic cooperation projects, can help create the conditions for a peaceful and prosperous coexistence between Israelis and Palestinians.

1.46 The importance of international support: International support is essential to promote a peaceful solution to the Israeli-Palestinian conflict. This includes political, financial and diplomatic support for peace and reconciliation initiatives, recognition of Palestinian and Israeli rights, and commitment to respect international law and human rights in the region. The involvement of the international community can help to create a favorable environment for dialogue and negotiation and to support efforts for a just and lasting peace in the region.

1.47 The challenge of radicalization and extremism: Radicalization and extremism represent a significant challenge to security and stability in the region. Alienation, desperation, and lack of prospects can fuel feelings of resentment and vengeance, leading to increased violence and extremism on both sides. Addressing the deep roots of radicalization requires a holistic approach that addresses underlying causes, including social marginalization, economic injustice and discrimination, and promotes constructive alternatives to violence and extremism.

1.48 Commitment to the rights of children and young people: Children and young people are particularly vulnerable to the devastating effects of the Israeli-Palestinian conflict. Many grow up in an environment of violence, fear and uncertainty, experiencing emotional and psychological trauma that can have long-term consequences on their well-being and development. Protecting the rights of children and young people, guaranteeing them a safe and inclusive education, a decent living environment and positive development opportunities, is essential to building lasting and sustainable peace in the region.

1.49 Humanitarian challenges in conflict areas: Civilian populations in conflict areas, both Israeli and Palestinian, face serious humanitarian challenges. Violence, blockade and movement restrictions have a devastating impact on their daily lives, with serious consequences for access to essential services such as drinking water, healthcare and education. International and local humanitarian organizations work to provide assistance and protection to those in need, but they face ongoing challenges in reaching the most vulnerable communities due to restrictions and unstable conditions on the ground.

1.50 The role of the international community in providing humanitarian assistance: The international community has a crucial role in providing humanitarian assistance to populations affected by the Israeli-Palestinian conflict. Organizations such as the International Committee of the Red Cross (ICRC), UNRWA and various NGOs work to ensure that those affected have access to basic services such as food, water, medical care and temporary housing. However, funding and resources for humanitarian assistance are often insufficient to meet the growing needs of populations affected by violence and forced displacement.

1.51 The challenge of gender-based violence in conflict: Women and girls in conflict areas face specific risks and serious human rights violations. Gender-based violence, including domestic violence, rape, and sexual violence, is widespread and is used as a weapon of war and social control. Women and girls are also often responsible for family support and face serious economic and social difficulties as a result of the conflict. Addressing gender-based violence and ensuring protection and assistance to women and girls in conflict areas is essential to promote justice and dignity for all.

1.52 Corporate responsibility in the conflict: Companies operating in the occupied Palestinian territories are often involved in violations of human rights and international laws. Companies that provide security services build illegal settlements or exploit natural resources in the occupied territories contribute to the perpetuation of the occupation and the violation of Palestinian rights. The responsibility of companies to respect human rights and international laws has been the subject of increasing attention from human rights organizations and the international community, and requires concrete measures to ensure that companies are not complicit in human rights violations in the occupied territories.

1.53 Initiatives of dialogue and reconciliation between communities: Despite divisions and tensions, there have been numerous initiatives of dialogue and reconciliation between the Israeli and Palestinian communities. These initiatives include meetings between religious leaders, intercultural dialogues, cultural exchanges, and joint community development projects. Although such initiatives may encounter resistance from extremists and radical groups, they are essential to promote mutual understanding, build bridges between communities, and create the basis for peaceful and prosperous coexistence in the region.

1.54 The need to address the deep roots of the conflict: To resolve the Israeli-Palestinian conflict in a lasting way, it is essential to address its deep roots, including the military occupation, the right of Palestinian refugees, the future of Jerusalem and the security of both sides. This requires sincere political commitment on the part of the Israeli and Palestinian leadership, as well as the support of the international community, to address these issues fairly and based on the principles of justice, dignity and human rights for all.

In conclusion, the Israeli-Palestinian conflict is extremely complex and rooted in a long and intricate history of rivalry, occupation, violence and human suffering. The reasons for the conflict are many and the solutions are immense and complex challenges that require political, social, economic and moral commitment on the part of all parties involved.
Addressing the deep roots of the conflict will require a holistic approach that addresses key issues such as military occupation, the right of Palestinian refugees, the future of Jerusalem, and the security of both sides. This requires an

open and constructive dialogue between Israelis and Palestinians, supported by the international community, to find balanced and just solutions that respect human rights and promote peace and prosperity for both communities.

At the same time, it is essential to address immediate humanitarian challenges in conflict areas, ensuring access to basic services such as water, medical care and education for civilian populations affected by violence and forced displacement. This requires an ongoing commitment on the part of international humanitarian organizations and the international community to provide assistance and protection to those in need.

Finally, it is essential to promote dialogue, reconciliation and mutual understanding between Israeli and Palestinian communities, creating spaces for open and constructive confrontation, the sharing of experiences and the construction of bridges of trust and solidarity. Only through a collective commitment to peace and justice, based on fundamental values of respect, equality and dignity for all, can we hope to overcome the Israeli-Palestinian conflict and build a better future for future generations.

2. Origins and ideology of Hamas.

Hamas, acronym for 'Harakat al-Muqawama al-Islamiyya' in Arabic, which means 'Islamic Resistance Movement', is a Palestinian political-military organization active in the Gaza Strip and other parts of the Palestinian territories. Hamas was founded in 1987 during the first intifada against the Israeli occupation and has emerged as one of the main Palestinian political and resistance organizations. Hamas' ideology is based on an extremist interpretation of Islam, combined with strong Palestinian nationalism. Hamas' stated goal is the creation of a Palestinian state based on Islamic law (Sharia) throughout historic Palestine, which includes present-day Israel. In addition, Hamas explicitly opposes the presence and existence of the State of Israel, considering it illegitimate and illegal.
Hamas has a long history of terrorist attacks against Israeli civilian targets, including suicide bombings, rocket

launches, and other violent actions. These attacks have been condemned by the international community as acts of terrorism. Hamas has been designated as a terrorist organization by many countries, including the United States, the European Union, and Israel. Its presence and activities are considered a threat to security and stability in the region.

Hamas was born as a wing of the organization of the Muslim Brotherhood in Palestine, but over the years it has developed its own identity and organizational structure. Initially, Hamas emerged as a popular resistance movement, offering social services, humanitarian assistance, and support to the families of the martyrs. This presence in the field has helped to gain consensus and popular support, especially among the most disadvantaged sections of Palestinian society.
One of Hamas' distinguishing characteristics has been its combination of

political and military activities. While participating in Palestinian democratic elections and gaining significant representation in the local government, Hamas has maintained an active armed wing, known as the al-Qassam Brigade, which has conducted military operations against Israel.

The organization has also developed a vast network of social institutions, including schools, hospitals, clinics and social care centers, which have helped to consolidate its support among the Palestinian population. These social services have been seen as a way to counter the influence of the corrupt and ineffective Palestinian government, improve people's living conditions, and promote Hamas' Islamic ideology.
Over the years, Hamas has faced significant challenges and changes. After winning the Palestinian parliamentary elections in 2006, Hamas took control of the Gaza Strip in 2007 after violent clashes

with the rival Fatah party, which controls the Palestinian Authority in the West Bank. This has led to a political divide between Gaza and the West Bank, with Hamas governing authoritatively in the Gaza Strip while Fatah remains in power in the West Bank.

In recent years, Hamas has tried to balance its military activities with political and diplomatic initiatives. He participated in various attempts at mediation and negotiations to reach a truce with Israel and resolve the Israeli-Palestinian conflict. However, his expansionist policies, refusal to recognize Israel, and his continued adherence to violence have hampered efforts for a peaceful and negotiated solution to the conflict.

Despite international pressure and challenges on the domestic front, Hamas remains a significant force in Palestinian politics and continues to exert considerable influence in the Gaza Strip. His Islamist ideology and his commitment to armed resistance against Israel represent an ongoing challenge to stability and security in the region.

Hamas emerged as a response to the Palestinians' frustration and desperation over the Israeli occupation and the lack of progress in peace negotiations. During the first intifada, growing Palestinian nationalist sentiment led to the formation of resistance groups, including Hamas, that tried to combat the Israeli occupation through armed resistance and the recruitment of followers based on a radical Islamic ideology.
The organization has evolved over the years, adopting a multifaceted approach to pursue its objectives. On the one hand, Hamas has continued to conduct attacks against Israel, including the firing of rockets from the Gaza Strip and terrorist attacks against Israeli civilian targets. On the other hand, it has developed a network of social services and charitable institutions to gain popular consensus and

support among the Palestinian population, especially in the occupied territories.

Hamas has also tried to position itself as an alternative to the Fatah-dominated Palestinian government, promoting a political agenda based on Islamist ideology and armed resistance against the Israeli occupation. His victory in the 2006 Palestinian parliamentary elections was a turning point, bringing Hamas to power and creating political tensions and internal conflicts between Hamas and Fatah. However, Hamas' control over the Gaza Strip has led to a series of challenges, including the Israeli and Egyptian blockade, which has limited access to goods and services for the local population and has contributed to a deterioration in socio-economic conditions in the region. In addition, Hamas has faced criticism for its authoritarian rule and for its repression of dissenting voices and human rights in the Gaza Strip.

In recent years, Hamas has tried to
diversify its strategies, seeking to improve
relations with other regional and
international actors, including some Arab
countries and Turkey. He also expressed
interest in indirect negotiations with Israel
to achieve a long-term truce and improve
living conditions in the Gaza Strip.
In addition, Hamas has tried to present
itself as a legitimate political actor,
participating in reconciliation talks with
Fatah and other Palestinian groups and
supporting initiatives for Palestinian
national unity. However, tensions between
Hamas and Fatah, together with
ideological divisions and a lack of mutual
trust, have hampered efforts for complete
reconciliation and for the formation of a
united Palestinian government.
In summary, Hamas remains a significant
political and military actor in the region,
with a profound impact on Palestinian
politics and the situation in the Israeli-
Palestinian conflict. Its ideological and
strategic evolution over the years reflects

the challenges and opportunities it faces in pursuing its objectives of resistance against the Israeli occupation and the achievement of Palestinian interests.

Hamas has roots that go deep into the history of Palestine, but it has gained significant notoriety and influence especially after its founding in 1987. Initially, Hamas was born as a response to the perceived growing dissatisfaction of the Palestinian population with the peace negotiations with Israel and the lack of tangible progress towards the creation of an independent Palestinian state.
Its main founder, Sheikh Ahmed Yassin, was a Palestinian spiritual leader and one of the founding members of the Muslim Brotherhood in Palestine. Hamas is based on a radical Islamic ideology, with the stated objective of freeing all of Palestine from the Israeli presence and establishing an Islamic state on land considered sacred.

Hamas has gained popular support by offering social services and humanitarian assistance to Palestinian communities, especially during times of crisis and conflict. It has established schools, hospitals, clinics and economic support programs, thus providing a social safety net for Palestinians affected by poverty, occupation and violence.

However, Hamas has also been criticized for its use of violence and terrorism as tools to achieve its political objectives. He has conducted numerous suicide bombings, shootings and rocket attacks against Israeli civilian targets, causing the death and injury of many innocent people. These actions have led to international condemnation and have helped to perpetuate the cycle of violence in the Israeli-Palestinian conflict.

Despite internal divisions between Hamas and other Palestinian groups, such as Fatah, and tensions with the international community, Hamas has remained a significant political and military force in the Gaza Strip and beyond. He maintained control of his support base thanks to his combination of charitable activities, armed resistance, and nationalist and religious rhetoric.

In recent years, Hamas has tried to balance its commitment to armed resistance with political and diplomatic initiatives. He participated in indirect talks with Israel and expressed interest in a long-term truce, while maintaining his ultimate goal of liberating all of Palestine. However, the challenges remain enormous and the situation remains extremely complex, with the need to address the deep roots of the conflict and find just and lasting solutions for all parties involved.

Hamas has roots that go deep into Palestinian history and society. It emerged in response to a number of factors, including the continued Israeli occupation of the Palestinian territories, the lack of progress in peace negotiations, and the growing dissatisfaction among the Palestinian population with the political and economic situation. The organization developed in a context of oppression and desperation, in which many Palestinians sought an alternative to traditional parties such as Fatah, which they perceived as incapable of guaranteeing their rights and well-being.

The movement found support especially among the most disadvantaged sections of Palestinian society, offering social services and humanitarian assistance that the Palestinian government was unable to effectively guarantee. This helped to consolidate popular consensus around Hamas, despite the fact that its armed resistance tactics were divisive and criticized by some sectors of Palestinian society and the international community.

Hamas has also played an important role in shaping the Palestinian national identity, promoting a vision of Islam as an integral part of the struggle for national liberation and social justice. He exploited religious and nationalist rhetoric to mobilize popular support and justify his actions against Israel.

The organization has also faced internal and external challenges over the years. Tensions with Fatah and other Palestinian groups have led to armed conflicts and political divisions, weakening internal cohesion and the ability to act as a united front against Israel. In addition, Hamas has been under pressure from the international community, which has designated it as a terrorist organization and has tried to isolate it politically and financially.
Despite these challenges, Hamas has maintained a strong presence in the Gaza Strip and has continued to exert significant influence on Palestinian politics. Its ability to adapt to changing political circumstances and to mobilize popular support remains a formidable force in the political landscape of Palestine. However,

his commitment to armed resistance and extremist rhetoric continue to hinder efforts for a peaceful solution to the Israeli-Palestinian conflict.

In conclusion, Hamas represents a significant political and military force in contemporary Palestine, with deep roots in Palestinian history and society. Born as a response to the frustration and desperation of Palestinians with regard to the Israeli occupation and the lack of progress in peace negotiations, Hamas has gained popular support by offering social services and humanitarian assistance, while maintaining a commitment to armed resistance against Israel.

However, the organization has faced internal and external challenges over the years, including conflicts with other Palestinian groups and pressure from the international community. Despite this, Hamas has maintained a strong presence in the Gaza Strip and has continued to exert significant influence on Palestinian politics.

The future of Hamas and the Israeli-Palestinian conflict remains uncertain and complex. While the organization has shown some flexibility and expressed interest in a long-term truce with Israel, its commitment to armed resistance and extremist rhetoric continue to constitute significant obstacles to efforts for a peaceful and negotiated solution to the conflict.

Addressing the deep roots of the conflict and finding just and lasting solutions will require sincere commitment on the part of all parties involved, including Hamas, together with the international community. Only through dialogue, negotiation and mutual respect for the rights and aspirations of both sides can we hope to achieve sustainable peace and lasting stability in the region.

3. Immediate cause of the current conflict.

The immediate cause of the ongoing conflict between Israel and Hamas can be identified in a series of events that have led to increased tensions and armed clashes between the two sides. One of the main triggers was the deterioration of relations between Israel and the Palestinians in East Jerusalem, in particular in Sheikh Jarrah and at the Esplanade of Mosques, also known as the Temple Mount for Jews, and Al-Aqsa for Muslims.
Tensions have grown following decisions by the Israeli authorities to evict Palestinian families from their homes in Sheikh Jarrah, a predominantly Palestinian neighborhood in East Jerusalem, to make room for Jewish settlements. These actions have been considered provocative and illegal by the international community and have led to protests and clashes between Palestinians and Israeli security forces.

In addition, during the Muslim holy month of Ramadan, there were repeated clashes at the Esplanade of Mosques between Muslim worshipers and Israeli security forces, in part because of restrictions on access imposed by the Israeli authorities and the fears of Palestinians regarding Israeli attempts to limit their right to prayer and access to holy places.

Tensions peaked when Hamas launched a series of rockets toward Jerusalem, in response to violence against Palestinians in Sheikh Jarrah and at the Esplanade of Mosques. These attacks have elicited a strong response from Israel, which has intensified its bombing of the Hamas-controlled Gaza Strip in response to rockets launched by the Palestinian militant group.

The situation has further deteriorated with the escalation of attacks and bombings on both sides, with casualties and destruction in both Gaza and Israel. The escalation of the conflict has been fueled by a combination of provocation, retaliation and revenge on both sides, creating a cycle of violence that is increasingly difficult to break.

Another key element that contributed to the immediate cause of the conflict was the Israeli authorities' decision to prevent access to holy places during Ramadan, a time of great importance for Muslims. This move sparked anger and indignation among Palestinians, who saw the action as a provocation and a violation of their religious rights.

Violent crackdowns by the Israeli police against Palestinian demonstrators, including faithful who were gathering to pray at the Esplanade of Mosques, have further increased tensions. The videos showing the Israeli police entering the mosque's courtyards with stun grenades and tear gas have sparked strong international condemnation and fueled outrage among Palestinians.

At the same time, on the other hand, the attacks of Palestinian militant groups, including Hamas, with rocket launches at Israeli cities, have triggered a quick and decisive response on the part of Israel. The escalation of Israeli air strikes on the Gaza Strip was a response to rocket provocations launched by Hamas, causing serious damage and civilian casualties in the area.

In addition, the lack of a political resolution to the problems afflicting the region must be considered. The Israeli-Palestinian conflict is characterized by decades of tension and violence, with numerous attempts at mediation and peace negotiations that have failed to reach a lasting solution. This lack of progress in negotiations has contributed to growing frustration and desperation among Palestinians, fueling the use of violence as a form of protest and resistance.
Finally, the wider geopolitical context of the region must be taken into account. Regional tensions, including the ongoing

situation in Syria, the growing involvement of Iran and the rivalry between Iran and Israel, have contributed to a climate of instability and uncertainty that has fueled the Israeli-Palestinian conflict.

In summary, the immediate cause of the ongoing conflict between Israel and Hamas can be attributed to a series of triggering events, including violent repression against Palestinians in East Jerusalem, rocket launches by Hamas and Israel's military response, as well as the lack of progress in peace negotiations and the unstable geopolitical environment in the region.

A crucial aspect that fueled the immediate cause of the conflict was the increasing polarization and radicalization of positions on both sides. Over the years, there has been an increase in nationalism and extremism among both Israelis and Palestinians, with radical groups gaining more and more power and influence. This climate of radicalization has made it more difficult to find compromises and peaceful solutions to the conflict.

In addition, the absence of strong political leadership and a shared vision for the future has contributed to a lack of mutual trust and has made it more difficult for the parties involved to take concrete actions to resolve the conflict. Political divisions within both communities, with rival factions seeking to maintain and consolidate their power, have hampered efforts for a negotiated and peaceful solution to the conflict.

Another significant factor was the perception of injustice and discrimination on the part of the Palestinians, both within the occupied territories themselves and against Israel. Israeli occupation policies, including military control of Palestinian territories and the construction of illegal settlements, have contributed to growing anger and frustration among Palestinians, fueling the use of violence as a means of resisting the occupation.

On the other hand, Israel has cited its security as one of the main reasons for its military actions against Gaza. Attacks by Palestinian militant groups, including rocket launches against Israeli cities, were considered a direct threat to the security and well-being of the Israeli people, which justified Israel's military responses to protect its citizens.

Finally, the role of the media and propaganda in perpetuating and amplifying the conflict must be emphasized. The divergent narratives presented by the Israeli and Palestinian media have helped to create a distorted perception of reality and to reinforce stereotypes and prejudices against the other. This fueled the cycle of violence and retaliation, causing the conflict to intensify more and more.

In conclusion, the immediate cause of the ongoing conflict between Israel and Hamas can be attributed to a number of factors, including the polarization and radicalization of positions, the lack of political leadership and a shared vision for the future, the perception of injustice and discrimination on both sides, and the role of the media and propaganda in perpetuating the conflict.

In addition, the immediate cause of the conflict between Israel and Hamas is multifactorial and complex. It includes a series of triggering events, including violence and tensions in East Jerusalem, rocket launches by Hamas, and Israel's military response. However, these events are only the tip of the iceberg of a series of larger factors that have contributed to increasing instability and the deterioration of relations between the two sides.

Political polarization and radicalization of positions, together with the lack of strong political leadership and the absence of a shared vision for the future, have made it more difficult to find compromises and peaceful solutions to the conflict. Internal divisions between both Israelis and Palestinians, together with the perception of injustice and discrimination on both sides, have fueled anger and frustration, increasing the propensity for violence and retaliation.

Furthermore, the role of the media and propaganda in perpetuating and amplifying the conflict cannot be underestimated. The diverging narratives presented by the Israeli and Palestinian media have helped to create a distorted perception of reality and to reinforce stereotypes and prejudices, further fueling the cycle of violence and retaliation. Addressing the immediate causes of the conflict will require a sincere commitment on the part of both sides and the international community to seek solutions that address the deep roots of the conflict and promote peace, security and justice for both peoples. Only through dialogue, negotiation and mutual respect for the rights and aspirations of both sides can we hope to achieve a lasting and sustainable solution to the Israeli-Palestinian conflict.

4. Military strategies and tactics used by both sides.

The military strategies and tactics used by both sides in the Israeli-Hamas conflict are varied and reflect the complexity of the ongoing armed confrontation.
On the Israeli side, key strategies include the use of air and technological superiority to conduct precision operations against military targets and Hamas' infrastructure. Israel has used its drones, combat aircraft, and missile defense systems to locate and target rocket launch locations, underground tunnels, weapons production sites, and Hamas military commands. Israel's stated goal is to protect its citizens and defuse Hamas' military capabilities.

In addition, Israel has implemented a policy of targeted bombing, trying to avoid civilian casualties, but focusing on damaging Hamas' military capabilities and infrastructure. However, despite efforts to minimize civilian casualties, Israeli bombings have caused a significant number of deaths and injuries among the Palestinian population, raising criticism and concerns about the excessive use of force.

On the part of Hamas, strategies and tactics include the launching of rockets and mortars at Israeli cities, in order to inflict material damage and cause panic among the Israeli civilian population. Hamas has used a wide range of rockets, including some with more advanced capabilities and greater ranges than in the past, increasing the range of its attack.

In addition, Hamas has exploited its asymmetric warfare capabilities, including the use of underground tunnels to infiltrate Israeli territory and conduct surprise attacks against Israeli defense forces. These tunnels have also been used to transport weapons and supplies, making it more difficult for Israel to prevent the smuggling of military materials into the Gaza Strip.

Hamas has also adopted a strategy of hiding and dispersing its military infrastructure and its fighters among the civilian population, trying to exploit the presence of civilians as human shields and making it more difficult for Israel to hit military targets without causing casualties among non-combatants.

Finally, both sides have used propaganda and psychological warfare to influence national and international public opinion and support their respective narratives of the conflict. Israel has tried to justify its attacks as a legitimate defense against Hamas' terrorism, while Hamas has tried to portray itself as a resistance force against the Israeli occupation and defender of the rights of the Palestinian people. In summary, the strategies and tactics used by both sides in the Israeli-Palestinian conflict reflect the complexity and brutality of the ongoing armed conflict, with both sides seeking to make the most of their capabilities and resources to pursue their objectives and interests. However, the human cost and devastation caused by this conflict remain high, with a devastating impact on the civilian population and on the stability of the region.

Both sides in the Israeli-Hamas conflict have adopted a series of military strategies and tactics to pursue their objectives and gain advantages on the battlefield.
On Israel's part, the main approach has been to use its military and technological superiority to conduct targeted operations against Hamas' infrastructure. This includes the use of drones, combat aircraft and guided missiles to locate and hit rocket launch sites, underground tunnels used by Hamas to smuggle weapons and military materials, as well as command and control posts of the militant organization.

Israel has also employed psychological warfare tactics, such as issuing preventive alerts through telephone calls and text messages to warn Palestinian residents of the impending attack, in order to minimize civilian casualties and isolate Hamas from popular support. In addition, Israel has used its Iron Dome missile defense to intercept and neutralize rockets launched from Gaza, trying to protect Israeli civilian areas from attacks.

On the other hand, Hamas has adopted a strategy of guerrilla warfare and asymmetric combat against Israel. This includes the firing of rockets and mortars at Israeli cities, with the aim of hitting civilian targets and causing panic and material damage. Hamas has also tried to exploit the terrain and urban environment of the Gaza Strip to hide its infrastructure and fighters, making it harder for Israel to locate and target them.

In addition, Hamas has continued to use underground tunnels as a key tactic to conduct surprise attacks against Israel, infiltrate Israeli territory, and smuggle weapons and supplies into the Gaza Strip. These tunnels were a main target of Israeli military operations, which sought to destroy them to reduce Hamas' ability to conduct attacks against Israel.

At the same time, Hamas has tried to exploit the presence of civilians as human shields, placing its military infrastructure and fighters in densely populated areas to minimize the risk of being hit by Israeli attacks and to fuel the narrative of Palestinian victimization in the eyes of the international community.

In conclusion, the strategies and tactics used by both sides in the Israeli-Palestinian conflict reflect the complexity and brutality of the ongoing armed confrontation. However, despite the efforts of both sides to pursue their military objectives, the human cost and the suffering of the civilian population remain high, with a devastating impact on the lives of those involved and on the stability of the region as a whole.

Both sides in the conflict have also used their resources and logistical capabilities to pursue their military strategies. Israel, for example, has a well-developed intelligence network that it uses to gather information on Hamas' activities and to identify military targets. This information is then used to plan and conduct targeted operations against infrastructure and members of Hamas.
Israel has also spent considerable financial resources to develop and maintain its advanced military technology, including the Iron Dome system, which has proven to be effective in protecting Israeli civilian areas from rockets launched from Gaza. In addition, Israel has used its economic superiority to maintain a capacity to mobilize and respond quickly to threats from the Gaza Strip.

On the other hand, Hamas has exploited its network of supporters and affiliates across Palestine and the Arab world to obtain weapons, funding and logistical support. Hamas has received financial and political support from some Arab states and organizations, which share its opposition to Israel and its commitment to resistance against the occupation.

In addition, Hamas has tried to mobilize the support of the Palestinian population through propaganda campaigns and nationalist and religious rhetoric. The organization has promoted a vision of Islam as an integral part of the struggle for national liberation and has used the rhetoric of resistance and the defense of Palestinian rights to gain popular consensus and support its goal of fighting Israel.

Hamas has also tried to diversify its sources of military supply, trying to obtain weapons and supplies from different sources, including criminal networks and smugglers. The organization has demonstrated some adaptability and resilience in replenishing its forces with weapons and military materials, despite Israel's efforts to interrupt the flow of weapons into the Gaza Strip.

In addition, both sides have harnessed the power of communication and media to influence national and international public opinion. Israel has tried to portray itself as a victim of Hamas' aggression and has provided information about its military operations through press releases and official briefings. Hamas, on the other hand, has tried to present itself as a resistance force against the Israeli occupation and has released images and videos of the consequences of the Israeli bombing on the Palestinian civilian population.

In summary, the strategies and tactics used by Israel and Hamas reflect the complexity and brutality of the Israeli-Palestinian conflict, with both sides seeking to make the most of their resources and capabilities to pursue their military objectives and gain advantages on the battlefield. However, despite the efforts of both sides to pursue their military objectives, the human cost and the suffering of the civilian population remain high, with a devastating impact on the lives of those involved and on the stability of the region as a whole.

In conclusion, the military strategies and tactics used by Israel and Hamas reflect the complexity and brutal reality of the Israeli-Palestinian conflict. Both sides have used their resources, capabilities, and strategic advantages to pursue their military objectives and gain advantages on the battlefield. Israel has used its technological, financial and logistical superiority to conduct targeted operations and protect its citizens, using its intelligence network and Iron Dome system to counter threats from the Gaza

Strip. Hamas, on the other hand, has adopted a strategy of guerrilla warfare and asymmetric combat, exploiting its network of supporters and affiliates to obtain weapons and funding and using rocket launch tactics and underground tunnels to target Israel and infiltrate its territory.

Despite efforts by both sides to pursue their military objectives, the human cost and the suffering of the civilian population remain high. Military operations have caused significant numbers of civilian casualties, material damage and human suffering, fueling the cycle of violence and retaliation that continues to perpetuate the conflict. Addressing the root causes of the conflict and finding a peaceful and lasting solution will require a sincere commitment on the part of both sides, together with the international community, to resolve disputes and build a peace based on justice, dignity and mutual respect for human rights.

5. Effects of the conflict on the civilian population.

The effects of the conflict between Israel and Hamas on the civilian population are extremely devastating and have a lasting impact on the lives of millions of people, both in Israel and in the Gaza Strip.
In Israel, rocket attacks launched from Gaza have caused fear, panic and trauma among the civilian population, especially in cities close to the Gaza Strip such as Sderot, Ashkelon and Be'er Sheva. The frequent attacks have forced people to seek makeshift shelters and adapt to a lifestyle constantly in the shadow of the threat. Alarm sirens, which warn of the need to seek shelter in the event of an imminent attack, have become an integral part of daily life for many Israelis, especially children.
The victims of rocket attacks, although relatively few thanks to the Iron Dome missile defense system and bomb shelters,

have nonetheless caused human losses and injuries, with long-term emotional and psychological consequences for the families involved. In addition, material damage to homes, public infrastructure and livelihoods has forced many people to live in precarious conditions and has compromised the economic stability of the affected communities.

In the Gaza Strip, intensive bombing conducted by Israel has caused wide-scale devastation, with serious damage to civilian infrastructure, including homes, schools, hospitals, water and electrical systems. Military operations have caused a high number of civilian casualties, including men, women and children, with tens of thousands of displaced people forced to seek refuge in emergency facilities or relatives' homes.
The population of Gaza has been exposed to extremely difficult living conditions, with severe shortages of food, drinking water, medical care and other basic needs.

Restrictions on humanitarian access and the closure of border crossings have further aggravated the humanitarian crisis, limiting humanitarian assistance and preventing people from escaping violence and suffering.

In addition, the conflict has had a profound psychological impact on the civilian population, with high levels of stress, anxiety, depression and emotional trauma among adults and especially among children, who have experienced extreme violence and loss. The unbearable living conditions and the absence of prospects for peace and security have contributed to a widespread sense of desperation and despair among the people of Gaza.

In conclusion, the conflict between Israel and Hamas has had devastating effects on the civilian population of both sides, causing deaths, injuries, destruction of infrastructure and human suffering on a vast scale. Addressing immediate humanitarian needs and finding a lasting political solution to the conflict remain crucial challenges to ensure the security and well-being of the civilian population in the region.

The effects of the conflict on the civilian population are profound and complex, affecting every aspect of daily life and leaving emotional, physical and social scars that will last for a long time.
In Israel, the relentless threat of rockets from Gaza has created a constant climate of fear and anxiety. Families live in constant fear of sudden attacks and are forced to seek shelter quickly every time the alarm goes off. Public and private structures have been adapted and reinforced to withstand attacks, and many communities close to the Gaza border have experienced a constant erosion of their quality of life. Children grow up with a level of stress and insecurity that is not normal for their age, and many adults

suffer from mental health problems related to chronic stress.

The material damage caused by rockets, although not comparable to the destruction in Gaza, still has a significant impact on the communities involved. Damaged homes must be repaired or rebuilt, schools and hospitals must be rebuilt, and public infrastructure must be restored. This requires significant economic and human resources and can have lasting effects on the local economy and social cohesion.

In the Gaza Strip, the effects of the conflict are much more devastating. The densely populated enclave suffered air and ground attacks that destroyed entire neighborhoods, causing thousands of deaths and injuries and leaving many families homeless and without means of livelihood. Vital infrastructure, such as electricity and water networks, hospitals and schools, has been severely damaged, leaving the population without access to essential services.

The humanitarian crisis in Gaza has been aggravated by restrictions on humanitarian access and emergency supplies imposed by Israel, which have hampered relief and reconstruction efforts. The lack of food, drinking water and medical care has caused serious suffering to the civilian population, especially children, the elderly and the sick. Despair and anger are growing among the people of Gaza, fueling feelings of helplessness and hopelessness.

In addition, the conflict had a lasting impact on the social and cultural fabric of Gaza, with an increase in political polarization and internal divisions. Violence and destruction have undermined confidence in the capacity of local institutions to protect and assist the population, fueling suspicion and mistrust among citizens.

In summary, the effects of the conflict on the civilian population are devastating and complex, with long-term consequences for the health, economy and social stability of the region. Addressing immediate humanitarian needs and finding a political solution to the conflict remain crucial challenges to ensure the well-being and security of the civilian population in the region.

The effects of the conflict on the civilian population are palpable not only in the physical and material damage, but also in the emotional and psychological wounds it leaves behind. In Israel, families live with constant uncertainty and the fear of being hit by rockets coming from Gaza. Schools, parks, and public places have bomb shelters, and alarm sirens have become a familiar sound. Children grow up with constant fear and must learn to manage the trauma that comes from being exposed to dangerous situations. Even adults are not immune to these fears, and many people suffer from anxiety disorders and PTSD (Post-Traumatic Stress Disorder) because of the constant threat.

The material damage caused by rockets has a significant economic impact, with many homes, businesses and public infrastructure damaged or destroyed. The communities near the Gaza border suffer particularly, with many economic activities suffering losses and many people losing their jobs as a result of the destruction. Rebuilding requires time and resources, and many people struggle to recover from the resulting financial losses and economic hardships.

In the Gaza Strip, the effects of the conflict are even more devastating. The densely populated enclave has experienced years of blockade and isolation, with limited access to food, water, medical care and other basic needs. Israeli bombings have destroyed homes, hospitals, schools and public infrastructure, leaving thousands of people without a roof over their heads and without access to essential services. Drinking water supplies have been damaged, causing serious public health problems and waterborne diseases.

In addition, violence and destruction have a lasting impact on the psyche of the people of Gaza. Many residents suffer emotional and psychological trauma due to the loss of loved ones, the destruction of their homes, and unbearable living conditions. Children are especially vulnerable, with high rates of PTSD, depression and anxiety among young people growing up in an environment of violence and instability.

The conflict also has a profound socio-cultural impact, undermining social cohesion and trust in local institutions. Internal divisions deepen and tensions increase, making it more difficult for the people of Gaza to find unity and solidarity in times of crisis. Despair and frustration fuel instability and insecurity, creating a vicious cycle of violence and suffering that seems to have no end.

In conclusion, the effects of the conflict on the civilian population are devastating and lasting, with long-term consequences for the health, economy and social stability of the region. The search for a political solution to the conflict remains essential to guarantee peace and security for all the peoples involved.

The effects of the conflict on the civilian population are intrinsically linked to the nature of the conflict itself and its prolonged duration over time. In Israel, families live with daily uncertainty and a constant fear of terrorist attacks. Alarm sirens warning of the imminent threat of rockets coming from Gaza become a daily routine, and people must learn to react quickly to seek shelter in bomb shelters. This state of constant anxiety creates a climate of widespread fear that permeates every aspect of daily life, affecting personal decisions, emotional well-being and family dynamics.

The material damage caused by rockets can be devastating, especially in communities close to the Gaza Strip. Homes and public infrastructure are being damaged or destroyed, forcing people to rebuild their lives from scratch. Businesses suffer economic losses and many people lose their jobs due to the destruction of business activities. Reconstruction requires significant time and resources, and many communities are facing serious economic and social difficulties in trying to recover and rebuild.

In the Gaza Strip, the effects of the conflict are even more serious. The population has been living under an Israeli blockade for many years, with limited access to food, drinking water, medical care and other basic resources. The Israeli bombings have caused extensive damage to infrastructure and vital resources, leaving many people without access to essential services and forced to live in extremely precarious conditions. The lack of resources and the constant state of emergency have led to serious public health problems and malnutrition, with many people struggling to meet the most basic needs.

The emotional and psychological wounds caused by the conflict are just as significant. The people of Gaza live in constant fear of imminent attacks, and constant fear has a profound impact on people's mental health and emotional well-being. Children grow up with deep trauma and insecurities, with high rates of PTSD, depression, and anxiety among young people living in an environment of violence and instability.

In addition, the conflict has a lasting social and cultural impact on the population of Gaza. Internal divisions deepen and social cohesion erodes, making it difficult for the population to find unity and solidarity in times of crisis. Despair and frustration fuel internal tensions and conflicts, creating an environment of instability and insecurity that seems to have no end.

In summary, the effects of the conflict on the civilian population are widespread and long-lasting, with serious consequences for the health, economy and social stability of the region. The search for a political solution to the conflict remains fundamental to guarantee the peace and well-being of all those involved.

In conclusion, the effects of the conflict on the civilian population are profound and lasting, with devastating consequences for the health, economy and social stability of the region. In Israel, families live with constant anxiety about rockets coming from Gaza, which threaten their security and emotional well-being. Material damage caused by rockets can lead to significant economic losses and the destruction of local communities, with a lasting impact on quality of life and social cohesion.

In the Gaza Strip, the effects of the conflict are even more devastating, with serious shortages of resources and essential services that strain the survival and well-being of the civilian population. The emotional and psychological wounds are deep and lasting, with childhood trauma affecting the mental health and emotional well-being of future generations. In addition, the conflict has a lasting social and cultural impact, undermining social cohesion and trust in local institutions. Addressing the effects of the conflict requires a long-term commitment to the reconstruction and healing of the communities involved, together with concerted efforts to find a political solution to the conflict itself. Peace and security in the region depend on the ability of all parties involved to work together to overcome divisions and build a future of stability and prosperity for all the peoples of the region.

6. Reactions of the international community to the conflict.

The reactions of the international community to the conflict between Israel and Hamas have been varied and have reflected the opinions, interests and alliances of the various global actors.

Some countries have expressed strong support for Israel, stressing its right to self-defense against terrorist attacks emanating from the Gaza Strip. These countries often condemn Hamas' actions as terrorism and stress the need to guarantee the security and safety of Israeli citizens. The United States, for example, has historically supported Israel and has provided military and political assistance to the Israeli government.

Other countries and international organizations have instead condemned the

Israeli attacks on Gaza, underlining the heavy toll paid by the Palestinian civilian population. These actors often call for an immediate ceasefire and demand respect for international humanitarian law on the part of both sides. In addition, many of them demand a political solution to the conflict that guarantees the human rights and self-determination of the Palestinian people.

Some states and organizations have tried to broker a diplomatic solution to the conflict, trying to negotiate a ceasefire and promoting dialogue between the parties. These efforts often face difficulties due to the complexity and sensitivity of the conflict, but they remain crucial to trying to end violence and start a lasting peace process.

In addition, the international community has played an important role in dealing with the humanitarian consequences of the conflict, providing humanitarian assistance, financial aid and support to international and non-governmental organizations operating in the field. However, the coordination and distribution of aid may be hampered by the situation on the ground and the restrictions on access imposed by both sides.

In summary, the reactions of the international community to the Israeli-Palestinian conflict have been complex and varied, reflecting the complexity and sensitivity of the conflict itself. While some countries openly support Israel or Palestinians, others are trying to broker a diplomatic solution and to provide humanitarian assistance to people affected by violence. However, the conflict remains one of the most urgent and divisive challenges in international politics, requiring a continuous and coordinated commitment on the part of all concerned actors to achieve a just and lasting peace in the region.

The reactions of the international community to the conflict between Israel and Hamas reflect a series of political, strategic and moral nuances that characterize international relations in the context of the Israeli-Palestinian conflict.

Some countries, especially those that have close historical and political ties with Israel, tend to openly support Israel's right to defense and condemn Hamas' actions as terrorism. These states often provide diplomatic and military support to Israel, underscoring its legitimacy as a sovereign state and its right to protect its citizens from terrorist attacks. Such positions may derive from strategic alliances, geopolitical interests, or historical and cultural solidarity with Israel.

On the other hand, there are countries and international organizations that openly criticize Israel's actions in the conflict, stressing the human cost and suffering of the Palestinian civilian population. These actors often denounce Israel's excessive use of force and demand strict respect for international humanitarian law, including the principle of proportionality in the use of force. Some of them may also support the recognition of Palestinian rights, including the right to self-determination and the creation of an independent state. Some states and international organizations have tried to act as mediators in the conflict, seeking to facilitate dialogue and negotiation between Israel and Hamas to achieve a sustainable ceasefire and initiate a meaningful peace process.

These efforts may involve direct diplomatic negotiations or the involvement of international mediators, such as the United Nations or other regional actors.

In addition, the international community plays an important role in providing humanitarian assistance to the civilian population affected by the conflict, through

the sending of financial aid, medical supplies and logistical support to humanitarian organizations and United Nations agencies. However, the coordination and distribution of such aid may be hampered by hostilities between warring parties and access restrictions imposed by Israel and Hamas.
In summary, the reactions of the international community to the Israeli-Palestinian conflict are characterized by a series of political, strategic and moral positions that reflect the complexity and sensitivity of the conflict itself. While some countries openly support Israel or the Palestinians, others seek to act as mediators or provide humanitarian assistance to the population affected by violence.

However, the conflict remains one of the most urgent and divisive challenges in international politics, requiring a continuous and coordinated commitment on the part of all concerned actors to achieve a just and lasting peace in the region.

The reactions of the international community to the conflict between Israel and Hamas represent a complex mosaic of opinions, policies and interests that reflect the diversity of the global landscape and the geopolitical dynamics of the Middle East region.

Some Western countries, especially the United States and many European states, have traditionally supported Israel as a key ally in the region. These countries often side with Israel, recognizing its right to self-defense and condemning Hamas' actions as terrorism. Western support for Israel can stem from a number of factors, including historical ties, shared values such as democracy and regional security.

On the other hand, many Muslim-majority countries and some non-aligned states tend to support the Palestinian cause and condemn Israel's actions as violations of international human rights.

These states often denounce the Israeli occupation of the Palestinian territories and demand respect for international humanitarian law. Support for the Palestinian cause may derive from religious, cultural considerations, or solidarity with oppressed peoples.

Other international actors, such as the United Nations and the European Union, have tried to act as mediators in the conflict, seeking to facilitate dialogue and negotiation between the parties to the conflict to achieve a peaceful and lasting solution. These efforts often focus on the importance of dialogue and diplomacy as a means of resolving disputes and promoting security and stability in the region.

In addition, the international community has played a key role in providing humanitarian assistance to the civilian population affected by the conflict, through the sending of financial aid, medical supplies and logistical support to humanitarian organizations and United Nations agencies. However, humanitarian efforts may be hampered by hostilities between warring parties and access restrictions imposed by both sides.

In summary, the reactions of the international community to the Israeli-Palestinian conflict reflect the complexity of global relations and the unique challenges associated with the conflict itself. While some countries openly support Israel or the Palestinians, others seek to act as mediators or provide humanitarian assistance to the population affected by violence. The conflict remains one of the most urgent and complex challenges in international politics, requiring a continuous commitment on the part of all interested actors to find a peaceful and lasting solution that guarantees peace and security for both parties involved.

In conclusion, the reactions of the international community to the conflict between Israel and Hamas reflect the diversity and complexity of global geopolitical dynamics. While some countries openly support Israel or the Palestinians, others seek to act as mediators or provide humanitarian assistance to the population affected by violence. However, the conflict remains one of the most urgent and complex challenges in international politics, requiring a continuous and coordinated commitment on the part of all interested actors to find a peaceful and lasting solution that guarantees peace and security for both parties involved. Addressing the conflict requires not only diplomatic commitment, but also strong support for the reconstruction and healing of affected communities, as well as respect for international law and fundamental human rights. Only through a collective and sustained commitment will it be possible to address the deep roots of the conflict and

work towards a solution that respects the
aspirations and rights of all those involved.

7. The role of media and propaganda in shaping perceptions of conflict.

The role of media and propaganda in shaping perceptions of the conflict between Israel and Hamas is crucial and complex, influencing national and international public opinion, politics, and the perception of justice and injustice.
The media play a fundamental role in telling the story of the conflict, but often the narratives are influenced by political, cultural and national biases. The media in Israel can focus on the narrative of security and the right to self-defense, highlighting terrorist attacks from Gaza and threats to the lives of Israeli citizens.

At the same time, the Palestinian media tend to emphasize the issue of occupation, discrimination and the suffering of the Palestinian population, stressing the human cost of Israeli military actions.

Propaganda is widely used by both sides to influence public opinion and justify their actions. Israel can use propaganda to legitimize military operations as necessary for national security and to portray Hamas as a terrorist organization that threatens the lives of Israelis. In the same way, Hamas can use propaganda to gain national and international support, portraying Israel as a colonial aggressor that oppresses the Palestinian people and violates their fundamental human rights.

Social media also plays an increasingly important role in shaping perceptions of conflict, allowing individuals to share news, images and opinions in real time. However, social media can also be used to spread disinformation and propaganda, amplifying existing tensions and divisions and making it difficult for the public to distinguish between facts and falsehoods.

Media coverage of the conflict may also be influenced by geopolitical and financial interests, with some media outlets that may have ties to pressure groups or governments that openly support one of the parties involved. This can lead to a distortion of the truth and a partial representation of the facts, making it difficult for the public to have a complete and balanced understanding of the conflict.

In conclusion, the role of media and propaganda in shaping perceptions of the conflict between Israel and Hamas is significant and complex. Media narratives and propaganda can influence public opinion and politics, fueling existing tensions and divisions. Addressing this challenge requires greater transparency, ethical and critical journalism, and media education that helps the public critically evaluate the information they receive.

The role of media and propaganda in the conflict between Israel and Hamas is intrinsic to the very nature of the conflict and reflects the complex political, social and cultural dynamics involved. The media, both traditional and digital, have an enormous influence in shaping public opinions and the global perception of conflict, and this happens through a series of communication mechanisms and strategies.

One of the most significant aspects of the media's role is the narrative of the conflict. Each party involved in the conflict tries to present their version of the events in order to obtain the support of national and international public opinion. The Israeli media tend to emphasize the threat of rockets coming from Gaza and Israel's right to self-defense, while the Palestinian media emphasize the suffering of the Palestinian civilian population and the resistance against the Israeli occupation.

Propaganda plays a key role in shaping the narrative of the conflict. Both sides use propaganda strategies to promote their political agenda and paint the other side as the enemy. Israel can use propaganda to portray Hamas as a terrorist organization that deliberately targets Israeli civilians, while Hamas can portray Israel as an aggressor that seeks to oppress the Palestinian people and usurp their lands.

Social media has further amplified the media's role in the conflict. Platforms such as Twitter, Facebook and Instagram allow individuals to share news, images and opinions in real time, reaching an immediate global audience. However, social media can also be fertile ground for the dissemination of misinformation and propaganda, as information is not always verified or thoroughly verified before being shared.
In addition, international media and news organizations may have implicit or explicit biases that influence their coverage of the conflict.

Some media may have political, financial or cultural ties with one of the parties involved, influencing their objectivity and impartiality in the narrative of the facts. In summary, the role of media and propaganda in the conflict between Israel and Hamas is complex and controversial. The narrative of the conflict is influenced by multiple factors, including political interests, national ideologies, and media biases.

Addressing this challenge requires ethical, critical and transparent journalism, as well as media education that helps the public to critically evaluate the information they receive and to understand the complexity of the conflict.

In conflicts such as that between Israel and Hamas, the role of the media and propaganda plays a crucial role in shaping public opinion and influencing the international perception of the conflict. The media, both traditional and digital, act as a bridge between field events and the global public, but they are often subject to political, cultural and financial influences that can distort the narrative of events.

One of the main ways in which the media influence the perception of conflict is through the selection and presentation of news. The choice of which stories to cover, which images to show, and which sources to cite can have a significant impact on public understanding of events. For example, media coverage that emphasizes Palestinian terrorist attacks may create a distorted perception of the threat to Israel's security, while coverage that highlights the suffering of Palestinians under Israeli occupation may bring out sympathy for the Palestinian cause.

Propaganda is another weapon used by warring parties to influence national and international public opinion. Israel and Hamas both use a variety of mediums, including press releases, videos, and social media, to promote their political agenda and portray the other side as the aggressor.

Propaganda can be accurate or distorted, depending on the objectives of the warring parties, and it can play a significant role in perpetuating the cycle of violence and revenge.

Social media has revolutionized the way in which conflict is told and perceived, allowing individuals and groups to share news, opinions and images in real time. However, social media can also be fertile ground for the dissemination of misinformation and propaganda, as information is not always verified or thoroughly verified before being shared.

This can lead to the spread of false narratives and the perpetuation of harmful stereotypes that further fuel conflict.

Infine, i media internazionali svolgono un ruolo chiave nel plasmare la percezione globale del conflitto. La copertura mediatica internazionale può avere un impatto significativo sulle relazioni diplomatiche e sulle azioni politiche dei governi nei confronti del conflitto.

Tuttavia, la copertura mediatica internazionale può anche essere influenzata da bias impliciti o espliciti, così come da pressioni politiche ed economiche che possono limitare la sua obiettività e indipendenza.

In conclusion, the role of media and propaganda in the conflict between Israel and Hamas is extremely complex and multidimensional. The narrative of the facts is subject to multiple influences and interests, which can distort the perception of the truth and further fuel the conflict. Addressing this challenge requires ethical, critical and independent journalism, as well as media education that helps the public critically evaluate the information they receive and understand the complexity of the conflict.

In conclusion, the role of media and propaganda in the conflict between Israel and Hamas is fundamental and complex, profoundly influencing the global perception of the conflict and national and international public opinions. The selection and presentation of news, together with the dissemination of propaganda by both parties to the conflict, can distort the perception of the truth and perpetuate the harmful stereotypes that further fuel the conflict. Social media has further amplified this role, allowing individuals and groups to share information and opinions in real time, but also facilitating the spread of misinformation and propaganda. Addressing this challenge requires ethical, independent and critical journalism, as well as media education that helps the public to critically evaluate the information they receive and to understand the

complexity of the conflict. Only through balanced information and an accurate understanding of the causes and implications of the conflict can one hope to promote a peaceful and lasting solution.
8. Attempts at mediation and peace negotiations.

Mediation attempts and peace negotiations in the Israeli-Hamas conflict have been frequent over the years, however, they have encountered numerous obstacles and have often led to limited or ephemeral results. One of the main challenges in peace negotiations is the lack of mutual trust between the parties. Israel and Hamas do not recognize each other's legitimacy and this makes it difficult to create common ground for dialogue. In addition, both sides have differing views on key issues, such as borders, mutual recognition, and the status of Jerusalem, which make it difficult to reach an agreement.

Some of the major mediation efforts have been conducted by regional and international actors, including the United States, the European Union, Egypt, and the United Nations. However, these efforts have often been met with resistance from warring parties or with a lack of political will on both sides to seriously engage in peace negotiations.

One of the biggest obstacles to the peace negotiations was the lack of unity among the Palestinians themselves. Israel has often maintained that it cannot negotiate with Hamas, an organization considered terrorist by many countries, and has preferred to deal with Mahmoud Abbas's Palestinian Authority, which controls the West Bank. However, the division between Gaza and the West Bank has made it difficult for Palestinians to present a unified position in peace negotiations.

Despite these obstacles, there have been some positive developments in attempts at mediation and peace negotiations. For example, in 2020, Egypt facilitated a ceasefire agreement between Israel and Hamas after a series of violent clashes. This agreement has led to relative calm in the region for several months, demonstrating that mediation can be successful in mitigating violence and stabilizing the situation.

However, mediation efforts and peace negotiations remain a complex and multilateral challenge. Achieving lasting peace will require continued commitment from all stakeholders, along with significant international support and an open and inclusive dialogue between all Palestinian and Israeli factions. Only through a process of sincere and inclusive negotiations can we hope to achieve a peaceful and lasting solution to the conflict between Israel and Hamas.

In conclusion, attempts at mediation and peace negotiations in the conflict between

Israel and Hamas have been characterized by numerous obstacles and challenges. The lack of mutual trust, differences on key issues, and lack of unity among the Palestinians themselves have made it difficult to reach a lasting agreement.

However, there has been some progress, such as the ceasefire agreements facilitated by Egypt, that have temporarily reduced violence in the region.
Addressing the complex roots of the conflict requires constant commitment from all parties involved, together with strong international support and an inclusive and open dialogue. It will be essential to overcome political and ideological differences and work together to address the concerns of both sides and ensure security and well-being for all the peoples of the region.

To achieve lasting peace, a multilateral approach will be needed that actively involves regional and international actors, as well as all Palestinian and Israeli factions. This will require a sincere and persistent commitment to seeking political and diplomatic solutions that respect the rights and aspirations of all parties involved.

In addition, it will be crucial to address the root causes of the conflict, including issues related to security, borders, the right to self-determination and human dignity. Only through a process of constructive and inclusive negotiations will it be possible to achieve a lasting peace and a just solution for all those involved in the conflict between Israel and Hamas.

9. Economic impact of the conflict on Gaza and Israel.

The conflict between Israel and Hamas has a significant economic impact on both sides involved, with negative consequences that extend beyond the direct material damage caused by the fighting.
For Gaza, a territory already heavily affected by years of economic blockade and isolation, the conflict involves serious damage to civil infrastructure, homes, businesses and productive resources. Israeli air strikes destroy or damage roads, schools, hospitals, power plants and water facilities, increasing the already serious humanitarian crisis in the Gaza Strip. The destruction of infrastructure makes it difficult to provide essential services such as drinking water and electricity, and local businesses struggle to survive in an environment of constant conflict.
On the other hand, Israel is also suffering a significant economic impact as a result of the conflict. Rocket attacks from Gaza

threaten the security of Israeli citizens and cause direct damage to homes, infrastructure and businesses in communities close to the Gaza Strip. In addition, constant fears of terrorist attacks and the need to respond militarily to rocket launches can create economic and social instability in the region.

In addition to direct material damage, the conflict has a negative impact on key sectors of the economy of both sides. Tourism, commerce, agriculture and industry are all affected by the disruptions caused by the fighting, the loss of investor confidence and the movement restrictions imposed by the authorities. In addition, the climate of instability and violence discourages foreign investment and damages the international image of both Gaza and Israel as safe destinations for trade and tourism.

Finally, conflict has a social and emotional impact on both communities, causing psychological stress, trauma, and loss of life. The loss of life and the suffering inflicted on families profoundly affect the social and psychological fabric of the communities involved, with long-term consequences on economic efficiency and social cohesion.

In conclusion, the conflict between Israel and Hamas has a significant economic impact on Gaza and Israel, with negative consequences that extend beyond the direct material damage caused by the fighting. Addressing the economic and social challenges caused by the conflict requires a joint commitment on the part of both sides, together with strong international support and with political and diplomatic solutions that aim at lasting peace in the region.

The conflict between Israel and Hamas has a complex and varied economic impact on both parties involved, affecting different sectors of the economy and having long-term consequences on the socio-economic development of the region.

In Gaza, the economic situation is particularly critical because of the recurring conflict and the blockade imposed by Israel. Before the conflict, Gaza was already plagued by a severe economic crisis, with high unemployment rates, widespread poverty and dependence on international humanitarian assistance. The conflict brings further devastation, damaging vital infrastructure such as roads, schools, hospitals, and water and energy supply facilities. Not only does this damage entail immediate repair costs, but it also has long-term effects on Gaza's ability to rebuild and develop economically.

Local businesses are particularly affected by the conflict, with many suffering physical damage or loss of equipment and raw materials as a result of the bombing. In addition, the situation of instability and violence discourages investment and hinders the development of new economic activities. The agricultural sector is particularly vulnerable, with much arable land damaged or destroyed during fighting, further reducing the sources of livelihood for the local population.

Israel is also suffering an economic impact from the conflict. Although the country has a more developed economy than Gaza, communities neighboring the Gaza Strip face serious economic challenges due to the constant threat of rockets and terrorist attacks. Local businesses may suffer physical damage and financial loss as a result of bombing, and the need to protect the civilian population involves additional costs for security forces and defense infrastructure.

In addition, the conflict has wider consequences on the Israeli economy, affecting the perception of foreign investors and the country's political stability. Episodes of violence can discourage investment and damage key sectors of the economy, such as tourism and international trade.

In addition, the military spending necessary to address the rocket threat and protect the civilian population involves significant costs for the Israeli government. In summary, the conflict between Israel and Hamas has a negative economic impact on both parties involved, damaging infrastructure, businesses and vital resources for the region's socio-economic development. Addressing these challenges will require a joint commitment on the part of both sides, together with strong international support and political and diplomatic solutions that aim at lasting peace and sustainable economic development in the region.

The conflict between Israel and Hamas has economic impacts that extend far beyond the physical and material damage caused by direct fighting. These impacts include loss of life, psychological trauma, destruction of infrastructure and productive resources, as well as long-term consequences on the region's economic and social development.

In particular, to fully understand the magnitude of the economic impact of the conflict, it is important to consider the already difficult socio-economic context in which both Gaza and Israel find themselves. Before the last conflict, Gaza was already one of the most densely populated and poorest areas in the world, with high unemployment rates, a weak economic infrastructure and a chronic dependence on humanitarian assistance. Gaza's economic situation has been further complicated by Israeli restrictions on the movement of people and goods across borders, which have severely limited economic and development opportunities.

For Israel, communities close to the Gaza Strip are often subject to rocket attacks and infiltration by Palestinian armed groups, which creates a climate of fear and uncertainty that can harm the economic and social well-being of these communities. In addition, the cost of the military operation itself, including the costs of ammunition, military equipment and the maintenance of security forces, can have a significant impact on Israel's public budget.

In terms of direct economic impact, physical damage to infrastructure, homes, businesses, and productive resources can be extensive and costly to repair. For example, the destruction of roads, bridges, power plants and water plants can paralyze the entire local economy and delay economic recovery for years after the conflict. In addition, loss of life and subsequent physical disability can deprive families of income and create additional economic and social burdens for society.

In addition, the conflict may have long-term consequences on investment attractiveness and on the business climate in the region. Domestic and foreign investors may be reluctant to engage in long-term economic projects in an unstable area subject to frequent episodes of violence.

This can lead to a slowdown in investment and economic development, with negative consequences on economic growth and employment.

Finally, the political and social instability generated by the conflict can fuel internal and external tensions, threatening the security and stability of the entire region. The conflict can polarize political opinions and radicalize the positions of the factions involved, making it even more difficult to find a political and diplomatic solution to the conflict. This cycle of violence and instability can damage the international image of Gaza and Israel as reliable trading partners and can reduce opportunities for economic cooperation and regional development.

In conclusion, the conflict between Israel and Hamas has extensive and complex economic impacts on both parties involved, affecting different sectors of the economy and having long-term consequences on the economic and social development of the region. Addressing these challenges will require a joint commitment from all stakeholders, together with strong international support and political and diplomatic solutions that aim at lasting peace and sustainable economic development in the region.

The conflict between Israel and Hamas has a complex and profound economic impact that goes beyond the mere assessment of the direct material damage caused by the fighting. It involves multiple dimensions of the economy and society, affecting both Gaza and Israel in different and sometimes unpredictable ways.

In Gaza, the conflict has a devastating impact on the territory's already fragile economy. The Gaza Strip has been subject to severe restrictions by Israel, which controls land, sea and air borders, and the conflict has further compromised its access to external resources and markets. Damage to vital infrastructure, such as water and electricity networks, roads and government buildings, makes it difficult to provide essential services and worsens the already difficult economic situation of the population.

Local businesses are particularly affected, with many suffering irreparable damage or significant financial loss as a result of the bombings. Sectors such as agriculture, fishing and commerce are particularly vulnerable, with the destruction of arable land, fishing boats and shops causing loss of income and jobs for the local population.

In addition, the conflict has a negative impact on the mental health and psychological well-being of the population. The trauma and stress caused by bombing, the loss of family and friends, and the constant fear of new attacks can have lasting effects on mental health and on the population's ability to recover and rebuild after the conflict.

Even for Israel, the conflict has significant economic consequences. Communities close to the Gaza Strip are particularly affected by the threat of rockets and terrorist attacks, which can damage local homes, infrastructure and businesses. In addition, the cost of military operations, including ammunition, equipment and the maintenance of security forces, can be very high and represent a significant financial burden for the Israeli government.

The conflict may also have wider consequences for the Israeli economy as a whole. The perception of foreign investors and political stability can be compromised by violence and instability, which can damage key sectors such as tourism, trade and foreign direct investment.

In summary, the conflict between Israel and Hamas has a profound and complex economic impact on both parties involved, affecting multiple dimensions of the economy and society. Addressing these challenges will require a joint commitment from all stakeholders, together with strong international support and political and diplomatic solutions that aim at lasting peace and sustainable economic development in the region.

In conclusion, the conflict between Israel and Hamas has a devastating economic impact on both parties involved, with extensive consequences that go beyond direct material damage. For Gaza, already afflicted by poverty and dependence on humanitarian assistance, the conflict brings additional damage to infrastructure, businesses and vital resources, aggravating

the economic and humanitarian crisis in
the Strip.

Local businesses, agriculture and
commerce are particularly affected, with
losses of income and jobs that further fuel
the desperation and economic insecurity of
the population.

Israel is also suffering a significant
economic impact, with communities close
to the Gaza Strip facing the constant threat
of rockets and terrorist attacks, and the
government facing the high costs of
military operations and the need to protect
the civilian population. In addition, the
instability generated by the conflict can
damage key sectors of the Israeli economy
and discourage investment and tourism.

Addressing these challenges requires a
joint commitment on the part of both
parties, together with strong international
support and political and diplomatic
solutions that aim at lasting peace and

sustainable economic development in the region. Only through cooperation and the search for peaceful solutions can we hope to overcome the divisions and suffering caused by the conflict and to build a better future for all those involved in the region. 10. Personal experiences of those living in the midst of conflict.

The personal experiences of those living in the midst of the Israeli-Hamas conflict are incredibly varied and complex, reflecting the diversity of perspectives, identities, and individual circumstances within the communities involved.

For residents of Gaza, the conflict represents a daily reality marked by constant fear and the trauma of bombing and military attacks. Families face the difficult choice between staying in their homes, exposing themselves to the risk of being hit by bombing, or seeking refuge in safer places, often crowded and overcrowded, such as schools or underground shelters. The constant sound of bombing, the mourning of the loss of friends and family, and the lack of personal security have a profound impact on the mental health and emotional well-being of those living in Gaza.

On the other hand, for residents of Israeli communities close to the Gaza Strip, the conflict brings a constant feeling of vulnerability and fear. The threat of rockets and terrorist attacks can cause constant stress and anxiety, limiting people's freedom of movement and sense of security. Families face the difficult balance between protecting themselves and their loved ones and continuing to live normal lives despite looming threats.

For both communities, conflict has a profound impact on personal relationships and social cohesion. Friendships and families can be divided by political and ideological divisions, with lasting

consequences on the social fabric and on mutual trust within communities.
In addition, conflict can affect education, work, and personal development opportunities for young people growing up in an environment of violence and instability. Schools may be closed or damaged during fighting, limiting access to education and learning. Employment opportunities may be limited due to the destruction of local businesses and the reduction of tourism and investment.

However, despite the challenges and difficulties, many people in the communities involved in the conflict also find ways to resist, adapt, and find hope and resilience in their daily lives. Family and community support networks, together with local and international humanitarian aid initiatives, can provide vital support to people affected by the conflict, helping to alleviate pain and promote the recovery and reconstruction of affected communities.

In conclusion, the personal experiences of those living in the midst of the Israeli-Hamas conflict are characterized by a wide range of emotions, challenges and hopes. Conflict has a profound and lasting impact on the lives of those involved, affecting their mental health, their emotional well-being, their personal relationships, and their opportunities for personal development and growth. Addressing the challenges of the conflict will require continued commitment from all parties involved, together with significant support from the international community, to promote lasting peace and social justice in the region.

In conclusion, the personal experiences of those living in the midst of the Israeli-Hamas conflict are imbued with emotional, physical and psychological complexity. For many, conflict represents a daily reality of fear, trauma and loss, with profound consequences on mental health, emotional well-being and personal relationships.

However, these experiences are also characterized by extraordinary resilience and a determination to persevere despite adversity.

In the midst of chaos and devastation, stories of hope and solidarity emerge, with individuals and communities coming together to support each other, protect the most vulnerable, and seek peace and reconciliation. There are countless examples of people who work tirelessly to promote dialogue, understanding and cooperation between communities involved in the conflict.

However, addressing the deep roots of the conflict and overcoming divisions will require a collective and ongoing commitment from all stakeholders, together with significant support from the international community. Only through mutual recognition, justice, understanding and reconciliation will it be possible to build a future of peace and prosperity for all those involved in the region.

The personal experiences of Gaza
residents, Israeli communities close to the
Gaza Strip, and those living in the midst of
the conflict testify to human complexity
and resilience in the face of adversity. Each
individual carries with them a unique and
precious story that deserves listening,
respect and support in the search for a
peaceful and lasting solution to the
conflict.

11. Long-term effects of the conflict on the region.

The long-term effects of the Israeli-Hamas conflict on the region are extremely complex and affect different aspects of society, economy, politics and security.

From an economic perspective, the conflict has a lasting negative impact on both parties involved. The destruction of infrastructure, productive resources and economic activities slows economic recovery and limits opportunities for development and growth. Conflict-affected communities can take years to fully rebuild their economies and return to a state of economic stability.

In addition, the conflict fuels political polarization and social instability in the region, creating deep divisions between communities and making it more difficult to find political and diplomatic solutions to the conflict. Internal and external tensions can undermine social and political cohesion, hindering the creation of a shared vision for the future of the region.

At the humanitarian level, the conflict leaves an indelible mark on the population, with long-term consequences on the mental health, emotional well-being and security of those involved. The trauma and stress caused by bombing and violence can persist for years after the end of the conflict, affecting the quality of life and the ability of people to recover and rebuild their lives.

In addition, the conflict can have lasting effects on the region's environment and natural resources. The destruction of infrastructure can cause significant environmental damage, including soil and water pollution, loss of biodiversity, and ecosystem degradation. These effects may have long-term consequences on human health, agriculture, and water supply in the region.

Finally, the conflict has significant geopolitical implications, affecting relations between Israel, neighboring countries and the international community. Regional tensions can be fueled by continued instability and violence, with the potential to trigger larger and more protracted conflicts in the region. In addition, the conflict may affect the foreign policies and national security of other countries, with long-term consequences on global geopolitical stability.

In conclusion, the long-term effects of the conflict between Israel and Hamas on the region are profound and complex, affecting different aspects of social, economic, political and environmental life. Addressing these challenges will require a collective and continuous commitment from all stakeholders, together with strong support from the international community, to promote lasting peace, social justice and sustainable development in the region.

The long-term effects of the Israeli-Hamas conflict in the region are far-reaching and complex, permeating multiple aspects of social, economic, political and environmental life. These effects are evident both in the communities directly involved in the conflict and in the region as a whole.

Economically, the conflict has a devastating impact on the region's economic prosperity. The destruction of fundamental infrastructures such as roads, government buildings, hospitals and energy plants significantly slows down the process of reconstruction and economic recovery. Financial resources that may have been invested in development projects are diverted to reconstruction and humanitarian support, thus limiting opportunities for long-term economic growth and socio-economic development.

In addition, the conflict perpetuates cycles of poverty and economic dependence. Families affected by violence often lose their livelihoods and access to essential services, with lasting negative effects on their economic and social well-being. Unemployment, already high before the conflict, is increasing further due to the destruction of businesses and sources of work, making it difficult for many people to provide for themselves and their families.

On the social front, conflict undermines community cohesion and fuels division and suspicion between ethnic, religious and political groups. The emotional and psychological wounds caused by conflict can last for generations, affecting interpersonal relationships, trust in political leadership, and the perception of social justice. In addition, violence and instability can increase the risk of radicalization and recruitment by extremist groups, threatening the security and stability of the region as a whole.

At the environmental level, the conflict has devastating effects on the local ecosystem. The destruction of infrastructure, the indiscriminate use of weapons and ammunition, and the contamination of soil and water resources have a lasting impact on biodiversity, air and water quality, and the ecological balance of the region. These effects can have long-term consequences on human health and agriculture, compromising food security and increasing the risk of diseases related to environmental pollution.

Finally, the conflict has significant geopolitical implications, affecting relations between Israel, neighboring countries and the international community. Regional tensions can fuel larger and protracted conflicts, threatening global peace and security. In addition, the conflict may affect the foreign policies and national security of other countries, with long-term consequences on geopolitical stability and international cooperation.

In conclusion, the long-term effects of the conflict between Israel and Hamas on the region are profound and widespread, affecting multiple aspects of socio-economic, political, environmental and geopolitical life. Addressing these challenges will require a collective and continuous commitment from all stakeholders, together with strong support from the international community, to promote lasting peace, social justice and sustainable development in the region. The long-term effects of the conflict between Israel and Hamas on the region are manifold and can be analyzed from different points of view. First of all, at the socio-economic level, the conflict has devastating consequences that extend well beyond the duration of the military clashes. The destruction of crucial infrastructure such as roads, schools, hospitals, and water and energy facilities creates a vacuum that takes years, if not decades, to fill. Repair and reconstruction require large financial investments, which can divert resources from other sectors such as health, education, and social and economic development.

In addition, the conflict fuels economic and social inequality. The most vulnerable people and communities, such as refugees, the disabled and the elderly, are often the most affected by violence and destruction. Loss of livelihood, forced displacement, and emotional trauma can lead to greater marginalization and poverty, creating cycles of vulnerability that can persist for many generations.
From an environmental perspective, the conflict has lasting impacts on the local ecosystem.

The contamination of soil and water by unexploded ordnance and chemicals can irreparably damage biodiversity and compromise food and water security in the region. In addition, the destruction of natural habitats and the loss of natural resources may have long-term consequences on the region's ability to support human and animal life.

On the political front, conflict can lead to increased instability and radicalization. Affected communities may feel abandoned by existing political institutions and seek more extreme alternatives. Extremist groups can exploit chaos and uncertainty to recruit new members and promote their violent agenda. This can lead to a perpetual cycle of violence and instability that undermines peace and security in the region.

Finally, the long-term effects of the conflict also extend to the international sphere. Regional tensions can affect diplomatic and commercial relations between neighboring countries and their allies. In addition, the conflict may have implications for the foreign policy and national security of other countries, with long-term consequences on global geopolitical stability.

In conclusion, the long-term effects of the conflict between Israel and Hamas on the region are complex and multiple, affecting multiple aspects of social, economic, political and environmental life.

Addressing these challenges requires continued commitment from all parties involved, together with significant support from the international community, to promote peace, stability and sustainable development in the region.

The long-term effects of the conflict between Israel and Hamas on the region can be analyzed from multiple perspectives, since they profoundly affect the lives of millions of people and have significant implications for the social, economic, political and environmental development of the region as a whole.

First, at the socio-economic level, conflict has a devastating impact on the stability and prosperity of the communities involved. The destruction of critical infrastructure, such as roads, bridges, government buildings and public service facilities, slows economic recovery and increases dependence on humanitarian assistance. Families and businesses affected by the damage can take years to recover, and many people may find themselves in chronic poverty due to the loss of livelihoods and housing.
In addition, the conflict has lasting effects on the mental and physical health of those involved. The psychological trauma caused by violence and loss can persist for years after the conflict ends, affecting quality of life and ability to face daily challenges. The lack of access to basic health services and the destruction of health infrastructure can

increase people's vulnerability to long-term illness and injury.

On the political level, the conflict fuels polarization and extremism, creating deep divisions within communities and hindering the search for peaceful and lasting solutions. Struggles for power and territorial control can fuel new cycles of violence and instability, undermining trust in the political process and weakening democratic institutions.

From an environmental perspective, the conflict has destructive impacts on local ecosystems and on the region's natural resources. The contamination of soil, water and air by unexploded ordnance and toxic chemicals can irreparably damage biodiversity and compromise food and water security in the region. The destruction of natural habitats and the loss of natural resources can have long-term consequences on the region's ability to support human and animal life.

Finally, at the geopolitical level, the conflict has significant implications for regional and international relations. Tensions between Israel and neighboring countries may affect the balance of power in the region and have long-term consequences on global security and stability. The foreign policies of other countries may be influenced by the dynamics of the conflict, with possible consequences for international cooperation and world peace.

In conclusion, the long-term effects of the conflict between Israel and Hamas on the region are profound and complex, affecting multiple aspects of social, economic, political and environmental life. Addressing these challenges requires continued commitment from all parties involved, together with significant support from the international community, to promote peace, stability and sustainable development in the region.

In conclusion, the long-term effects of the conflict between Israel and Hamas on the region are extremely complex and profoundly affect the lives of those involved and the development of the region as a whole. These effects are manifested on multiple fronts, from the economy to politics, from health to the environment, creating lasting challenges that require continuous and sustained commitment to be effectively addressed.

At the socio-economic level, the conflict leads to a disintegration of social and economic structures, with consequences that last for years after the end of the fighting. The destruction of infrastructure, loss of lives and livelihoods, and political instability undermine communities' ability to rebuild and progress, contributing to a vicious cycle of poverty and dependence.

On the political front, the conflict fuels polarization and extremism, hindering the search for peaceful solutions and the construction of democratic and inclusive institutions. The lack of mutual trust and political will can lead to a perpetuation of the conflict and to further violations of human rights and civil liberties.

From an environmental point of view, the conflict has devastating effects on local ecosystems and natural resources, compromising the region's capacity to support human and animal life in the long term. The contamination of soil, water and air, together with the loss of natural habitats, threatens biodiversity and the region's food and water security.

Finally, at the geopolitical level, the conflict has significant implications for the security and stability of the region and the world. Tensions between Israel and neighboring countries may affect the balance of power in the region and have long-term consequences for global peace and international cooperation.

Addressing the long-term effects of the conflict requires continued commitment from all parties involved, together with significant support from the international community. Only through inclusive dialogue, cooperation and the search for peaceful solutions can we hope to overcome the divisions and suffering caused by the conflict and to build a better future for all those involved in the region.

12. Perspectives for a peaceful and sustainable solution.

The prospects for a peaceful and sustainable solution to the conflict between Israel and Hamas require a comprehensive, multilateral approach that addresses the deep roots of the conflict and promotes dialogue, mutual understanding and cooperation between all parties involved. Here are some key elements that could contribute to such a solution:

1. Dialogue and Negotiations: It is essential to engage in constructive dialogue and third-party mediated negotiations to address the concerns and aspirations of both parties to the conflict. This may include issues such as territorial boundaries, security, human rights and the self-determination of peoples.

2. Respect for international law: All parties involved must commit to respect international humanitarian law and human rights, including obligations deriving from the Geneva Conventions and United Nations resolutions. This includes the protection of civilians, the prohibition of indiscriminate attacks and an end to the illegal occupation of territories.

3. Building trust: It is necessary to create mechanisms and institutions that foster mutual trust between Israel and Hamas. This could include measures to ensure border security, the cessation of hostilities, the exchange of prisoners and the improvement of living conditions in the Gaza Strip.

4. Intra-Palestinian reconciliation: The movement toward a peaceful solution also requires a commitment to intra-Palestinian reconciliation between Hamas and Fatah. This could involve the formation of a Palestinian national unity

government that represents all Palestinians and can negotiate with Israel in a unified manner.

5. Investments in economic and social development: To sustain lasting peace, it is necessary to invest in infrastructure, education, health and economic development in the region. This can help improve the living conditions of the population and reduce the social and economic tensions that fuel the conflict.

6. Involving the international community: The international community must play an active role in facilitating dialogue and negotiation between Israel and Hamas. This could include diplomatic support, humanitarian assistance and economic development, as well as overseeing and monitoring the implementation of any peace agreements.

7. Long-term vision: It is important that all parties involved in the conflict adopt a

long-term vision and commit to lasting peace based on justice, equality and mutual respect. This requires a profound cultural and political change that can overcome the divisions and prejudices of the past.

In conclusion, a peaceful and sustainable solution to the conflict between Israel and Hamas is possible only through dialogue, mutual respect and commitment to address the root causes of the conflict. An inclusive and multilateral approach is needed that involves all stakeholders and promotes a shared vision for a future of peace and prosperity in the region.

To further outline the prospects for a peaceful and sustainable solution to the Israeli-Hamas conflict, it is essential to consider various factors and approaches that could contribute to achieving that objective.

1. Civil society involvement: The active involvement of civil society, including

religious groups, non-governmental organizations, and human rights activists, can play a significant role in promoting dialogue, mutual understanding, and peacebuilding. The participation of local communities and marginalized groups in defining solutions can guarantee greater legitimacy and sustainability of peace processes.

2. Gradual approach: A peaceful solution to the conflict often requires a gradual and flexible approach that takes into account the different opinions, interests and concerns of the parties involved. This could involve setting short- and long-term goals, with concrete measures to address the most pressing issues and building trust over time.

3. Respect for national aspirations and human rights: Any peaceful solution must respect the national aspirations and fundamental rights of all people involved in the conflict, including the right to self-

determination and security. This requires a commitment to social justice, equality and respect for the human rights of everyone, regardless of their ethnicity, religion or political affiliation.

4. Approach based on the principles of justice and forgiveness: A crucial element in building peace is the promotion of a culture of justice and forgiveness that allows communities to face the past and be reconciled with it. This may involve creating transitional justice mechanisms, such as truth and reconciliation commissions, that allow victims to tell their stories and perpetrators of human rights violations to take responsibility for their actions.

5. Development of democratic and inclusive institutions: A peaceful solution requires the development of democratic and inclusive institutions that represent and respect the diverse identities and opinions present in the region. This may

include constitutional reforms, free and transparent elections, and the strengthening of the rule of law and democratic institutions.

6. International support: The international community must continue to play an active role in supporting peace processes and in providing humanitarian assistance and economic development to the region. This could include financial, technical and political support for peace negotiations, as well as monitoring and evaluating the implementation of the agreements reached.

In conclusion, the prospects for a peaceful and sustainable solution to the conflict between Israel and Hamas are complex and require a multifaceted approach that considers the different dimensions of the conflict and actively involves all interested parties. Only through constant commitment and constructive dialogue is it possible to hope to overcome divisions and build lasting peace in the region.

Continuing the analysis of the prospects for a peaceful and sustainable solution to the conflict between Israel and Hamas, we can explore additional considerations and strategies that could contribute to achieving this objective.

7. Reducing tensions and building trust: It is crucial to take steps to reduce tensions and build trust between conflicting parties. This could include the cessation of military attacks and retaliatory operations, the release of political prisoners and the guarantee of humanitarian access to the inhabitants of Gaza. The creation of buffer zones or early warning mechanisms could help prevent the escalation of hostilities.

8. Inclusion of women and young people: Actively involving women and young people in decision-making and peace processes can lead to more inclusive and

sustainable solutions. Women and young people can bring diverse perspectives and creative innovations to resolve conflicts and promote peace at local and national levels.

9. Political and economic reforms: Implementing political and economic reforms can help create conditions for lasting peace. This could include promoting transparency, accountability and good governance, as well as measures to combat corruption and reduce socio-economic inequalities. Investments in education, vocational training and youth employment can reduce social and economic tensions and promote long-term stability.

In conclusion, the prospects for a peaceful and sustainable solution to the conflict between Israel and Hamas are complex and challenging, but not impossible to achieve. It is clear that dealing with the conflict will require a constant and coordinated commitment from all parties involved, as well as significant support from the international community. It is crucial to adopt a comprehensive, multilateral approach that addresses the root causes of conflict and promotes justice, equality and mutual respect.

This means engaging in constructive dialogue and negotiations mediated by third parties, while respecting the national aspirations and fundamental rights of all those involved in the conflict. It also means investing in reducing tensions, building trust and including women and young people in peace processes. In addition, it is essential to promote political and economic reforms, to support the reconstruction and socio-economic development of the region, and to promote education for peace and tolerance.

Only through constant commitment and effective cooperation is it possible to hope to overcome divisions and build lasting peace in the region. It is important that all parties involved maintain a sincere commitment to a peaceful solution, setting aside differences and working together for the common good. With determination, tolerance and political will, a peaceful solution to the conflict between Israel and Hamas can become a reality, benefiting not only the populations involved, but the entire region and beyond.

7. Role of international organizations in conflict management.

The role of international organizations in managing the conflict between Israel and Hamas is of fundamental importance for promoting peace, protecting human rights and providing humanitarian assistance to populations affected by the conflict. Here are some of the main contributions from international organizations:

1. Mediation and negotiation: International organizations, such as the United Nations and the European Union, can play a key role in mediation and negotiations to resolve the conflict. They can facilitate dialogue between conflicting parties, offer neutral platforms for negotiations, and provide technical assistance to develop peaceful and sustainable solutions.

2. Monitoring and observation: International organizations can play an important role in monitoring compliance

with international humanitarian law and human rights during the conflict. They may send field observation missions to gather information on alleged abuses and violations and to pressure warring parties to end violations and protect civilians.

3. Humanitarian assistance: International organizations, including UNRWA (United Nations Agency for Palestinian Refugees) and the ICRC (International Committee of the Red Cross), provide vital humanitarian assistance to populations affected by the conflict. They can distribute food aid, provide emergency medical care, guarantee access to drinking water, and provide shelter and protection for displaced civilians.

4. Crisis management: International organizations can play a key role in managing humanitarian crises and responding quickly to emergencies. They can coordinate relief efforts, mobilize financial and technical resources, and

ensure a fair and effective distribution of humanitarian aid.

5. Promotion of peace and reconciliation: International organizations can support peace and reconciliation initiatives between communities involved in the conflict. They can promote intercultural dialogue, support educational programs for peace and tolerance, and facilitate meetings between community representatives to promote mutual understanding and peaceful coexistence.

6. Strengthening institutions: International organizations can support the strengthening of democratic institutions, respect for the rule of law, and good governance in the region. They can provide technical and financial assistance to improve governance, promote transparency and accountability, and protect the fundamental rights of citizens. In conclusion, the role of international organizations in managing the conflict

between Israel and Hamas is crucial to promote peace, protect civilians and provide humanitarian assistance to affected populations. Through mediation and negotiations, monitoring and observation, humanitarian assistance, crisis management, promoting peace and reconciliation, and strengthening institutions, international organizations can contribute significantly to efforts to resolve the conflict and build lasting peace in the region.

In conclusion, the role of international organizations in managing the conflict between Israel and Hamas is essential to address humanitarian challenges, promote peace and ensure respect for international law. However, it is important to recognize that the success of international organizations' initiatives depends on the cooperation and political will of the parties involved in the conflict.
International organizations must continue to play an active role in promoting

dialogue, mediation and negotiations between Israel and Hamas, encouraging both parties to commit to an inclusive and sustainable peace process. At the same time, they must continue to monitor respect for international humanitarian law and human rights, reporting violations and providing humanitarian assistance to populations affected by the conflict.
In addition, international organizations must support reconciliation and peacebuilding initiatives at the local and national levels, promoting mutual understanding, tolerance and peaceful coexistence between communities involved in the conflict. They must also work with regional and international actors to address the root causes of the conflict and promote a political solution that respects the aspirations of both sides.
However, it is important to recognize that the role of international organizations has its limitations and that the solution to the conflict requires sincere commitment and political will on the part of all parties

involved. Only through a multilateral and inclusive approach, involving all stakeholders and addressing the root causes of the conflict, can we hope to achieve lasting peace in the region.

The involvement of international organizations in managing the conflict between Israel and Hamas represents an important pillar for the peaceful and sustainable resolution of the conflict. However, their role is only part of a larger picture that requires unprecedented global commitment and international cooperation.
International organizations must continue to play a proactive role in facilitating dialogue, mediation and negotiations between conflicting parties, encouraging an inclusive and multilateral approach that takes into account the legitimate aspirations of both parties. At the same time, they must strengthen their efforts to monitor and report violations of international humanitarian law and

human rights, ensuring the protection of civilians and providing humanitarian assistance to communities affected by the conflict.

However, to ensure the success of such initiatives, the full support and cooperation of all parties involved in the conflict is crucial.

7. Reactions of the Palestinian and Israeli diaspora to the conflict.

The reactions of the Palestinian and Israeli diaspora to the Israeli-Hamas conflict reflect a diverse range of opinions, sentiments and political positions. Here are some of the highlights of their reactions:

1. Palestinian diaspora:

• Solidarity and support: Many members of the Palestinian diaspora express solidarity and support for the Palestinian people, condemning the Israeli occupation and military actions in Palestine. This support can be manifested through protests, fundraisers for displaced persons and victims of the conflict, awareness campaigns and advocacy at the international level.

• Anger and frustration: The Palestinian diaspora may feel anger and frustration at the continuing violations of human rights and living conditions under the Israeli occupation. Israeli military actions against Gaza and other Palestinian areas further fuel this anger and frustration, prompting some members of the diaspora to mobilize and act to defend the rights of the Palestinian people.

• Call for justice and rights: Many members of the Palestinian diaspora demand justice, rights and self-determination for the Palestinian people. They support the need for a political solution that puts an end to Israeli occupation and colonization and that guarantees the right of return of Palestinian refugees and the creation of an independent Palestinian state.

2. Israeli diaspora:

• Supporting Israel's security: Many members of the Israeli diaspora express support for Israel's security and its defense against rockets launched by Hamas and other Palestinian organizations. They justify Israel's military actions as necessary to protect the country from security dangers and to ensure the survival of the Israeli people.

• Security concern: Some members of the Israeli diaspora may be concerned about the safety of their family members and friends in Israel, especially during periods of escalating conflict. They can support the Israeli government's actions in protecting the civilian population and ensuring the country's security.

• Criticism of the government: However, there are also members of the Israeli diaspora who criticize the Israeli government's policies towards the Palestinians and the conflict in general. They can support initiatives for peace, dialogue and reconciliation between Israelis and Palestinians, and they can oppose the occupation and colonization of Palestinian territories.

In conclusion, the reactions of the Palestinian and Israeli diaspora to the conflict reflect a complex range of perspectives and positions. While some express solidarity and support for their people, others seek to promote peace and justice through inter-community dialogue and collaboration. However, both the Palestinian and Israeli diasporas play a significant role in shaping public debate and influencing national and international policies regarding the conflict.

15. Analysis of previous treaties and agreements that have influenced the current situation.

The analysis of previous treaties and agreements that influenced the current situation in the conflict between Israel and Hamas provides an important framework for understanding the dynamics of the conflict and its origins. Here is an overview of the main treaties and agreements that have influenced the current situation:

1. Balfour Declaration (1917): This statement, issued by the British government during World War I, expressed British support for the establishment of a "national home for the Jewish people" in Palestine. This laid the foundation for the Zionist movement and contributed to the Jewish colonization of Palestine.

2. British Mandate of Palestine (1922-1948): The British Mandate established by

the League of Nations gave the United
Kingdom the administration of Palestine
after World War I. This has led to tensions
between the Jewish and Arab populations
in Palestine and to increasing violence.

3. United Nations Partition Plan (1947):
This plan proposed the division of
Palestine into two states, one Jewish and
one Arab, with Jerusalem as an
international city. Although accepted by
Jews, it was rejected by Arab states and led
to the 1948 Arab-Israeli War and the
Palestinian Exodus (Nakba).

4. 1949 Armistice: After the 1948 war,
armistice agreements were signed between
Israel and neighboring Arab countries
(Egypt, Jordan, Syria, and Lebanon).
These agreements outlined temporary
ceasefire lines, but they did not resolve the
fundamental issues of the conflict.

5. United Nations Security Council
Resolution 242 (1967): This resolution,

adopted after the 1967 Six-Day War, emphasized the principle of Israel's 'withdrawal from occupied lands' in exchange for 'recognition of the sovereignty, territorial integrity and political independence of all states in the region and their right to live in peace within secure and recognized borders'.

6. Oslo Accords (1993-1995): These Oslo agreements established a peace process between Israel and the Palestine Liberation Organization (PLO), providing for Palestinian autonomy in the occupied territories through the establishment of the Palestinian Authority. However, the peace process has run aground and has not led to a definitive solution to the conflict.

7. Camp David peace plan (2000): This plan, negotiated between Israel and the Palestinian Authority with the mediation of the United States, sought to resolve the fundamental issues of the conflict, including the status of Jerusalem, the final

borders, and the return of Palestinian refugees. However, the negotiations failed and led to an increase in violence.

8. Unilateral withdrawal from Gaza (2005): Israel evacuated Israeli settlers and withdrew military forces from the Gaza Strip in 2005. However, this withdrawal did not lead to lasting peace and instead fueled tensions between Israel and Hamas, which took control of the Gaza Strip.
These treaties and agreements have helped to shape the current situation in the conflict between Israel and Hamas, but they have also highlighted the persistent challenges in achieving a lasting peace and a political solution to the conflict.

In conclusion, the analysis of the previous treaties and agreements that have influenced the current situation in the conflict between Israel and Hamas highlights the complexity and persistence of the challenges in achieving a peaceful and sustainable solution to the conflict. Although these treaties and agreements attempted to address the fundamental issues of the conflict, such as the withdrawal of occupied lands, mutual recognition, and the creation of a Palestinian state, many of them failed to achieve lasting peace.

The failure to fully implement peace agreements, violations of international humanitarian law and human rights on both sides, the escalation of violence, and the absence of an effective negotiation process have all contributed to keeping the conflict in a state of stalemate and instability.

In addition, the lack of mutual trust between the parties, the presence of external actors with diverging interests in the region and the deep political and social divisions have further complicated the peace process.

To face these challenges and move towards a peaceful solution, a renewed commitment from all parties involved, the support of the international community and an approach based on respect for international law, human rights and the legitimate aspirations of both populations involved in the conflict will be necessary. Only through an inclusive negotiation process, a commitment to building trust and political will on the part of all the protagonists will it be possible to achieve a lasting peace and a political solution that respects the rights and aspirations of all the peoples of the region.

16. Role of the United States and other world powers in the conflict.

The role of the United States and other world powers in the conflict between Israel and Hamas has been significant and complex over the years. Here's an overview of the role they played:

1. United States:

• Military and economic support for Israel: The United States has been a strong supporter of Israel, providing considerable military and economic assistance. This support includes advanced weapons, financial aid, and diplomatic protection.

• Mediation and facilitation of peace negotiations: The United States has often tried to mediate peace negotiations between Israel and its neighbors, including the Palestinian Authority. However, the results of those efforts have been variable and no significant progress has been made toward a lasting solution.

• Supporting Israel's security: The United States has supported Israel's right to self-defense and has justified its military actions as a response to security dangers. However, there has also been criticism of the United States for its unconditional support for Israel and for its lack of impartiality towards the conflict.

2. European Union (EU):

• Promotion of the two-state solution: The EU has actively supported a two-state solution to the Israeli-Palestinian conflict, which involves the creation of an independent Palestinian state alongside Israel. It supported peace negotiations and provided economic and humanitarian assistance to the Palestinians.

• Criticism of human rights violations: The EU has openly criticized violations of human rights and international humanitarian law by both sides in the conflict, including the expansion of Israeli settlements in the occupied Palestinian territories and the excessive use of force against Palestinian civilians.

3. Other world powers:

• Russia: Russia played a marginal role in the conflict, occasionally offering diplomatic support and hosting meetings between the parties involved in the conflict. However, its role has generally been limited compared to the United States and the EU.

• Arab nations: Arab nations have played an important role in supporting the Palestinian cause and in promoting peace initiatives through the Arab League and other regional forums. However, their efforts have not always been coordinated and the conflict remains a divisive issue within the Arab world.

In conclusion, the United States and other world powers have influenced the conflict between Israel and Hamas through their political, military and economic support, their diplomatic efforts, and their role in shaping the international framework. However, the lack of a lasting solution and the persistence of tensions in the conflict indicate the complexity and challenge in finding a peaceful resolution that meets the needs and aspirations of both parties involved.

The United States and other world powers have had a significant impact on the conflict between Israel and Hamas, affecting not only the course of events on the ground, but also peace negotiations and the international framework as a whole.

The United States, in particular, has played a central role in supporting Israel. This support was evident through military and economic assistance, which helped to consolidate Israel's position as one of the region's leading military powers. This support has often been the subject of criticism, especially from Arab countries and many international observers, who have seen it as an obstacle to peace and as a perpetuation of the status quo.

However, the United States has not limited itself to supporting Israel. They have also played a mediating role in attempts to negotiate a solution to the conflict. Several U.S. administrations have tried to facilitate peace negotiations between Israel and the Palestinians, with mixed results. For example, the Oslo process in the 90s saw an active involvement of the United States as a mediator, while in the following years there were other attempts to restart peace negotiations, often without lasting success. Outside the United States, the European Union has played an important role in promoting the two-state solution and in supporting Palestinian autonomy through economic and humanitarian assistance.

However, like the United States, the EU has had difficulty translating this support into tangible progress towards peace, given the complexity of the conflict and the lack of political will on both sides.

At the same time, other world powers such as Russia have tried to play a mediating role in the conflict, although their impact has been limited compared to the United States and the EU.

In conclusion, the role of the United States and other world powers in the conflict between Israel and Hamas has been complex and controversial. Although they played an important role in shaping events on the ground and in peace negotiations, the persistent challenges in achieving a lasting solution indicate the complexity of the conflict and the need for continued commitment by the international community.

The United States and other world powers have influenced the conflict between Israel and Hamas in different and complex ways over the years. To fully understand their role, it is necessary to take a closer look at some of the key aspects of this dynamic.

1. Military and economic support for Israel: The United States has maintained strong military and economic support to Israel, providing advanced weapons, funding, and diplomatic protection. This support has been a constant in the relationship between the two countries and has had a significant impact on Israel's defense capabilities in the conflict with Hamas. However, such support has also drawn criticism from those who believe that the United States should be more committed to promoting peace and human rights in the region.

2. Mediating and negotiating role: The United States has often tried to play a mediating role in peace negotiations

between Israel and the Palestinians. These efforts were evident in several initiatives, such as the Oslo process in the 90s and the Camp David peace negotiations in 2000. However, despite efforts, no lasting agreement has been reached, and the role of the United States has often been the subject of controversy and criticism from both sides.

3. Political positions and national interests: The positions of the United States in the Israeli-Palestinian conflict are often influenced by its national interests and internal political dynamics. While some U.S. governments have adopted a policy more favorable to Israel, others have tried to adopt a more balanced position and promote a negotiated solution to the conflict. However, the consistency and effectiveness of those efforts have often been questioned.

4. Role of the European Union and other world powers: Other world powers, such as

members of the European Union, have also played an important role in the conflict, supporting the two-state solution and providing economic and humanitarian assistance to the Palestinians. However, the lack of unity and coordination between world powers has limited their effectiveness in promoting peace in the region.

In summary, the role of the United States and other world powers in the conflict between Israel and Hamas has been complex and influenced by a number of factors, including political and economic support for Israel, mediation and negotiation efforts, national political positions, and strategic interests. However, despite efforts, the conflict remains unresolved and peace continues to escape the region.

The United States and other world powers have played a leading role in the conflict between Israel and Hamas, with an impact that spans multiple political, economic and military aspects. One of the central elements of international involvement was the United States' support for Israel, which had a significant influence on the course of the conflict.

U.S. support for Israel has deep historical roots, with political, economic and military ties that go back many decades. This support has translated into advanced arms supplies, substantial financial aid, and diplomatic protection. The United States has often justified this support as an expression of solidarity with a democratic ally in the region and as a guarantee of Israel's security in a hostile geopolitical environment.

However, U.S. support for Israel has been criticized by those who support Palestinian rights and promote a negotiated solution to the conflict. These critics accuse the United States of favouritism towards Israel and of having helped to perpetuate the occupation of the Palestinian territories and the violation of human rights.

In addition to direct support for Israel, the United States has also played an important role in attempts to negotiate a solution to the conflict. In the 90s, they supported the Oslo process, which led to the signing of the Oslo Accords between Israel and the Palestine Liberation Organization (PLO). However, the Oslo process failed to bring about a lasting peace, and the conflict continued with periods of escalation and failed negotiations.

In addition to the United States, other world powers, including the European Union (EU), have tried to play a role in promoting peace in the Israeli-Palestinian conflict. The EU has supported a two-state solution, which involves the creation of an independent Palestinian state alongside Israel. However, the EU's efforts have often been limited by a lack of internal cohesion and the difficulty in coordinating a common response to the complex situation in the region.

In addition, other world powers such as Russia and some Arab nations have played a mediating role and supporting peace negotiations. However, the involvement of these powers has often been limited by diverging national and regional interests, which have made it difficult to reach a consensus on how to deal with the conflict. In summary, the role of the United States and other world powers in the conflict between Israel and Hamas has been extremely complex and controversial. While U.S. support for Israel has been a constant over the years, international efforts to promote a peaceful and negotiated solution to the conflict have been hampered by a lack of cohesion and political will on the part of world powers.

In conclusion, the involvement of the United States and other world powers in the conflict between Israel and Hamas had a significant impact on the course of events in the region. United States support for Israel has helped to strengthen Israel's position in the conflict and to guarantee its security, but it has also aroused criticism for alleged favouritism and for supporting policies considered contrary to Palestinian human rights.

However, international efforts to promote peace and a negotiated solution to the conflict have often been frustrated by a lack of cohesion and political will on the part of world powers. The complexity of regional dynamics, the diverging interest of world powers and the lack of mutual trust between the parties have made it difficult to reach a consensus on how to deal with the conflict.

In this context, the conflict between Israel and Hamas continues to persist, with periods of escalation of violence followed by attempts at mediation and negotiation. However, the lack of a political solution and the persistence of tensions in the conflict indicate the complexity and challenge in achieving lasting peace and a solution that meets the needs and aspirations of both parties involved.

17. Possible regional implications of the conflict.

The possible regional implications of the Israeli-Hamas conflict are diverse and complex, with the potential to affect the balance of power, stability, and security across the Middle East region. Some of these implications include:

1. Regional destabilization: The conflict between Israel and Hamas can contribute to the destabilization of the region, fueling ethnic, religious, and political tensions that extend beyond the borders of Israel and the Gaza Strip. This instability can fuel internal conflicts in neighboring countries and influence wider regional dynamics.

2. Radicalization and extremism: Conflict can fuel radicalization and extremism across the region, fueling resentment against Israel and its supporters. This can lead to increased terrorist activities and the

proliferation of extremist groups that seek to exploit the conflict for their own ends.

3. Challenges to the stability of neighboring countries: Neighboring countries, such as Egypt, Jordan and Lebanon, may be affected by instability and violence that spread across borders during periods of conflict escalation. This can strain the internal stability of these countries and create challenges for the security of their borders.

4. Regional tensions: The conflict may increase regional tensions between Israel and its Arab neighbors, as well as between Arab countries themselves. Arab countries' reactions to the conflict may vary, with some openly supporting Hamas and others maintaining diplomatic relations with Israel. These tensions can have a significant impact on regional geopolitical dynamics and on diplomatic relations.

5. Changes in the geopolitical framework: The conflict can lead to changes in the region's geopolitical framework, with consequences for regional and international alliances. For example, it may affect relations between Israel and countries such as Saudi Arabia, the United Arab Emirates, and other Gulf states, which may see conflict as a determining factor in their security strategies and foreign policy.

6. Economic implications: The conflict may have significant economic implications for the region, with damage to infrastructure, business interruptions, and economic losses. This may aggravate existing economic challenges in the countries involved in the conflict and have negative repercussions on the regional economy as a whole.

In summary, the regional implications of the conflict between Israel and Hamas are complex and can have significant consequences for the stability, security, and economy of the Middle East region. It is essential to address the conflict in a comprehensive and multilateral manner, involving all interested regional and international actors, in order to mitigate its negative consequences and work towards a peaceful and lasting solution.

The regional implications of the Israeli-Hamas conflict can be further explored by considering the specific dynamics of certain countries and groups within the Middle East region.
First, Egypt plays a key role in managing the conflict, as it borders the Gaza Strip and has a long history of mediating between Israel and Hamas. Egypt has often played a mediating role in times of crisis between the two sides, trying to negotiate ceasefires and peace negotiations.
However, the Egyptian leadership must also face internal challenges related to the security of the border with Gaza and the

prevention of the onset of Islamic extremism in Sinai.

Jordan, another neighbor of Israel, has a significant population of Palestinian origin and has an interest in maintaining stability in the region. The conflict between Israel and Hamas may have an impact on Jordan's internal stability, as tensions in the conflict can fuel resentment among Jordanian Palestinians and influence the domestic political debate.

In Lebanon, the militant group Hezbollah has a close relationship with Hamas and may be involved in the conflict in a variety of ways. Hezbollah can provide logistical and military support to Hamas during armed conflicts with Israel, increasing the risk of a greater escalation of the conflict in the region. In addition, Hezbollah's involvement may also further complicate international and regional mediation efforts to resolve the conflict.

At the same time, the conflict between Israel and Hamas may influence the internal political dynamics of other countries in the region, such as Syria and Iraq, where militant groups and external actors may seek to exploit the conflict to promote their interests. In addition, the regional implications of the conflict may extend to relations between Israel and other Arab states, such as Saudi Arabia and the United Arab Emirates, which may be influenced by public reactions to Israel's management of the conflict and by the region's wider geopolitical dynamics.

In summary, the regional implications of the conflict between Israel and Hamas are complex and interconnected, affecting a range of political, economic, and security actors and dynamics across the Middle East region. Fully understanding these implications requires a detailed analysis of the internal relationships and dynamics of each country, as well as of the interactions between regional and international actors involved in the conflict.

In addition to the actors directly involved in the Israeli-Hamas conflict, such as Israel itself, Hamas, and the Palestinian population, it is important to consider the involvement of other nations and groups in the Middle East region and beyond.
For example, Iran played a significant role in the conflict, providing financial, logistical and military support to Hamas. Iran sees Hamas as a key ally in its strategy of countering Israel and in its effort to extend its influence in the region. Iran's support for Hamas may further fuel the conflict and increase the risk of further escalation.

In the same way, other regional actors such as Turkey can influence the conflict through their political and diplomatic support for Hamas. Turkey has tried to exploit the conflict to promote its strategic interests and to consolidate its position in the region. Turkey's involvement may have significant implications for the dynamics of the conflict and for mediation and negotiation efforts.

Saudi Arabia and other Gulf states may also play a role in the conflict, either directly through their financial support for the Palestinians, or indirectly through their political and diplomatic influence in the region. Although these states have shown some degree of solidarity with the Palestinian cause, their geopolitical interests may also lead them to seek a balance between supporting the Palestinians and maintaining relations with Israel and the United States.

In addition, the conflict between Israel and Hamas may have global implications, affecting the international relations and foreign policy of other countries outside the region. For example, Europe and the United States may be called upon to play a more active role in promoting a peaceful solution to the conflict and in providing humanitarian assistance to Palestinians affected by the conflict.

In summary, the regional and global implications of the conflict between Israel and Hamas are extremely complex and interconnected, involving a wide range of geopolitical actors and interests. Fully understanding these implications requires a detailed analysis of regional and global dynamics and of the interactions between the actors involved in the conflict.

In addition to the involvement of individual regional and global actors, it is also important to consider the dynamics of international organizations and political blocs in the context of the conflict between Israel and Hamas.

The United Nations plays a central role in monitoring the humanitarian situation in the Gaza Strip and the occupied Palestinian territories, as well as in promoting a negotiated solution to the conflict. UNRWA (United Nations Agency for Palestine Refugees) provides humanitarian assistance and basic services to the Palestinian population, while the United Nations Security Council is tasked with addressing security issues related to the conflict and promoting peace and security in the region.

The European Union (EU) has also played a significant role in the conflict, providing economic and humanitarian assistance to the Palestinians and supporting a two-state solution as a way to resolve the conflict. However, the EU has also found itself divided on some issues related to the conflict, with some member states supporting a more critical position towards Israel and others maintaining closer relations with the Israeli government. Similarly, other regional actors such as the Arab League and the Organization of Islamic Cooperation (OIC) have tried to play a role in promoting peace and security in the region. However, internal divisions between the members of these bodies may limit their effectiveness in promoting a resolution of the conflict.

Finally, it is important to consider the role of regional and global political blocs in the context of the conflict. For example, the Non-Aligned Movement and the Group of 77 supported the Palestinian cause and sought to promote a negotiated solution to the conflict. Likewise, the G7 and other Western political blocs supported Israel and tried to influence the resolution of the conflict through their political and diplomatic support.

In summary, the involvement of international organizations and political blocs in the conflict between Israel and Hamas reflects the complexity and interconnectedness of regional and global dynamics that influence the resolution of the conflict. Fully understanding the role of these actors requires a detailed analysis of their policies, their priorities, and their interactions with other actors involved in the conflict.

International organizations, such as the Red Cross and the International

Committee of the Red Cross (ICRC), play a critical role in providing humanitarian assistance during the conflict between Israel and Hamas. These organizations focus on medical assistance, food relief and assistance to refugees, working to alleviate the suffering of the civilian population affected by the conflict.

The Red Cross and the ICRC operate independently of governments and groups in conflict, following the principles of neutrality, impartiality and independence. This allows them to access conflict-affected areas and to provide humanitarian assistance to people in need, regardless of their political or religious affiliation.

Humanitarian assistance activities include providing emergency medical care, distributing food and drinking water, ensuring access to basic health services, and protecting civilians from serious violations of international humanitarian

law, such as indiscriminate attacks and violence against non-combatants.
In addition, international humanitarian organizations, such as Doctors Without Borders (MSF) and Oxfam, play a key role in providing medical and social assistance to Palestinians affected by the conflict.

These organizations work to ensure that the humanitarian needs of the civilian population are met and to promote respect for human rights and international humanitarian law.
However, humanitarian organizations often face significant challenges in providing assistance during conflict, including obstacles to access, lack of resources, and risk to humanitarian personnel. Armed conflict can make access to affected areas dangerous, putting both humanitarian workers and people in need of assistance at risk.

In addition, humanitarian organizations may be subject to deliberate attacks or restrictions by groups in conflict, which may prevent or limit their ability to operate effectively. This can seriously compromise their ability to provide vital assistance to civilians affected by the conflict.

Despite these challenges, the humanitarian assistance provided by international organizations remains crucial to mitigate the suffering of the civilian population during the conflict between Israel and Hamas. The protection of civilians and respect for international humanitarian law should be a top priority for all parties involved in the conflict, in order to ensure that the most vulnerable people receive the help they desperately need.

In addition to humanitarian organizations, it is important to consider the role of international financial institutions during the conflict between Israel and Hamas. These institutions, such as the International Monetary Fund (IMF) and the World Bank, play a fundamental role in providing economic assistance and in rebuilding infrastructure in territories affected by the conflict.

The IMF and the World Bank provide funding and technical assistance to help countries mitigate the negative economic effects of the conflict, promoting economic stability and sustainable growth. This may include financing economic development programs, debt restructuring, and supporting structural reforms to improve economic governance.

During the conflict between Israel and Hamas, the IMF and the World Bank can play a crucial role in providing financial and technical assistance to the Palestinian population to help them recover from the devastating effects of the conflict. This may include supporting the healthcare sector, rebuilding destroyed infrastructure, and supporting local businesses to resume economic activities.

However, international financial institutions may also face challenges in providing assistance during conflict, including the need to ensure that funds are used effectively and transparently and that they reach those who need them most. The conflict can also complicate the distribution of assistance and the monitoring of development programs, due to access restrictions and lack of security. In addition, international financial institutions may be subject to political pressure from different parties involved in the conflict, which may influence decisions on resource allocation and economic policies. It is crucial that the IMF and the World Bank maintain their independence and impartiality in providing assistance during the conflict, ensuring that the needs of the civilian population are at the center of their priorities.

In summary, the role of international financial institutions during the conflict between Israel and Hamas is crucial to guarantee economic support and reconstruction in the territories affected by the conflict. However, these institutions face significant challenges in providing assistance in a context of armed conflict, including obstacles to access and political pressure.

In addition to humanitarian organizations and international financial institutions, it is also important to consider the role of non-governmental organizations (NGOs) during the conflict between Israel and Hamas.

NGOs play a fundamental role in providing direct assistance to the civilian population during the conflict, often filling the gaps left by state and international institutions. These organizations may operate in areas where government and international agencies have difficulty accessing, offering a wide range of humanitarian and development services.

NGO activities during the conflict may include providing medical and psychological care to the wounded and traumatized, distributing food and basic necessities to affected families, providing educational assistance and helping to rebuild destroyed infrastructure. In addition, NGOs play a crucial role in monitoring respect for human rights and international humanitarian law by all parties involved in the conflict and in advocating for the protection of civilians.

During the conflict between Israel and Hamas, local and international NGOs can play a key role in providing assistance to the Palestinian population in the Gaza Strip and other conflict-affected areas. These organizations often operate under extremely difficult conditions, facing obstacles to access, security threats, and political pressure from various actors involved in the conflict.

However, despite the challenges, the role of NGOs during the conflict is crucial to ensure that the humanitarian needs of the civilian population are met and that human rights are respected. It is crucial that NGOs maintain their independence and neutrality, operating impartially to provide assistance to those who need it most, regardless of their political or religious affiliation.

In summary, NGOs play an essential role in providing humanitarian and development assistance during the conflict between Israel and Hamas, ensuring that the needs of the civilian population are met and that human rights are respected. Despite the challenges, these organizations continue to work with dedication and commitment to alleviate the suffering of those affected by the conflict.
In addition to humanitarian organizations, international financial institutions and non-governmental organizations (NGOs), it is also important to consider the role of solidarity networks and grassroots initiatives in the context of the conflict between Israel and Hamas.

Solidarity networks can emerge at the local, national and international levels in response to the conflict, uniting individuals, groups and communities that share a common commitment to supporting the affected population and promoting peace and justice. These networks can organize fundraisers, awareness campaigns, peaceful protests and other actions to make their voices heard and support those most affected by the conflict.

Basic initiatives, on the other hand, can be initiated by individuals or small groups who wish to do their part to alleviate the suffering of the civilian population and promote peace in the region. These initiatives may include the collection of basic necessities, the provision of direct assistance to affected families, the promotion of intercultural and interreligious dialogue, and other concrete actions to promote understanding and reconciliation between groups in conflict.

Solidarity networks and grassroots initiatives can play an important role in the context of the conflict between Israel and

Hamas, providing tangible support to the affected population and promoting greater civil commitment to peace and justice. These initiatives can help to raise public awareness of the causes and consequences of the conflict, encourage solidarity between people of different nationalities, ethnicities and religions, and promote an approach based on human rights and non-violence to conflict resolution.

However, it is important to recognize that solidarity networks and grassroots initiatives can also face challenges in the context of the conflict, including repression by the authorities, threats to security, and lack of resources and support. Despite these challenges, the role of these initiatives in building peace and promoting human rights and social justice cannot be underestimated, and their presence and continued commitment are essential to building a future of peace and prosperity in the region.

In conclusion, solidarity networks and grassroots initiatives play a vital role in the context of the conflict between Israel and Hamas, offering practical and moral support to the affected civilian population and promoting a civil commitment to peace and justice. These networks and initiatives embody the empathy, solidarity and determination of individuals and communities around the world in seeking to alleviate human suffering and promote a culture of peace and non-violence. However, to maximize the impact of these solidarity initiatives and networks, it is essential that they receive support and recognition from the international community, governments and institutions. This may include financial support, legal and political protection, as well as the promotion of education and public awareness of the causes and consequences of the conflict.

In addition, it is important that solidarity networks and grassroots initiatives remain rooted in the principles of non-violence, respect for human rights and peacebuilding. Only through an ongoing and unified commitment to peace and justice can these networks help create the foundation for a brighter and more equitable future for everyone in the Middle East region.

Ultimately, solidarity networks and grassroots initiatives bear witness to human ingenuity and resilience, offering hope and support to those suffering in the context of the Israeli-Hamas conflict and working tirelessly to build a better world for future generations.

18. Stories of refugees and those displaced by the conflict.

The stories of refugees and those displaced by the conflict between Israel and Hamas offer a valuable perspective on direct human experiences and the devastating consequences of the conflict. These stories testify to the pain, loss and resilience of those involved, highlighting the challenges faced by the affected communities and their desire for peace and a decent life. Refugees and displaced persons can come from a wide range of backgrounds, including refugee camps in the Gaza Strip and the West Bank, as well as from communities affected by bombing and military operations. Their stories may vary widely, but they often share common elements of desperation, family separation, loss of homes and livelihoods, as well as the struggle to access basic services such as food, drinking water, and healthcare.

The stories of refugees and displaced persons can also reveal the psychological and emotional trauma caused by the conflict, including post-traumatic stress disorder, depression and anxiety. These experiences can leave a lasting impression on those affected, affecting their mental health, emotional well-being and interpersonal relationships.

However, despite the challenges faced, the stories of refugees and displaced persons can also inspire hope and resilience. Many people affected by the conflict demonstrate an extraordinary capacity for adaptation and a determination to rebuild their lives and communities. Through mutual support, solidarity and community mobilization, many people find the strength to face adversity and to pursue a better future for themselves and their loved ones.

In addition, the stories of refugees and displaced persons can play a crucial role in raising public awareness and policy makers about the human consequences of the conflict and the need for effective and sustainable humanitarian responses. These stories can help break stereotypes and prejudices against refugees and migrants, promoting greater understanding and solidarity with them.

Ultimately, the stories of refugees and displaced persons offer a powerful testimony to direct human experiences of the conflict between Israel and Hamas, highlighting the urgent need for peaceful, sustainable, and human rights-based solutions to end suffering and promote peace and stability in the region.

19. Role of natural and territorial resources in perpetuating conflict.

The role of natural and territorial resources in perpetuating the conflict between Israel and Hamas is complex and multifaceted, with multiple factors contributing to tension and instability in the region.
First, the control of water resources is a significant source of conflict in the region. Water scarcity is a crucial challenge in the Middle East, and controlling water resources can be vital to the security and well-being of a population. In territories such as the West Bank and the Gaza Strip, Israel's control of water resources has raised tensions, with accusations of discrimination in access to water and in the distribution of resources.
Second, control of territories is a source of persistent conflict. Israel maintains strong control over the occupied territories, including the West Bank and East Jerusalem, while Hamas governs the Gaza

Strip. Territorial disputes, including issues related to borders, illegal settlements and the right of return of Palestinian refugees, remain unresolved issues that fuel the conflict.

In addition, natural resources, such as natural gas off the coast of Gaza, can be a factor of contention. Disputes over the exploitation of these resources and over property rights can increase tensions between Israel and Hamas, further complicating the search for a peaceful solution to the conflict.

Natural and territorial resources act as levers of power and control for both parties involved in the conflict. Their exploitation and management influence the dynamics of power, access to resources and the quality of life of the people involved. However, as long as these issues remain unresolved and contested, they will continue to fuel tension and instability in the region.

Addressing issues related to natural and territorial resources requires a multilateral and cooperative approach, involving all stakeholders and aimed at an equitable and sustainable management of shared resources and territories. Only through dialogue, negotiation and respect for the rights of all the communities involved can we hope to end the conflict and promote lasting peace and stability in the region.

Natural and territorial resources are at the center of the conflict between Israel and Hamas and play a significant role in perpetuating tensions in the Middle East region.
A critical aspect concerns the control of water, a vital resource for human survival and economic development. In the Middle East, water resource management has historically been the subject of controversy and conflict. Israel controls much of the region's water resources, including the Jordan River and West Bank aquifers. This

control has led to disparity in access to water between Israelis and Palestinians, fueling resentment and tension.

In addition, the territory itself is a reason for conflict. The West Bank, East Jerusalem and the Gaza Strip are all contested areas, with Israel extending its sovereignty over part of these territories through military occupation. Israeli settlements in the West Bank have been a source of tension, as they are considered illegal under international law and undermine the prospects for a two-state solution.

Even natural resources such as natural gas can fuel the conflict. The gas field off the coast of Gaza has been the subject of disputes between Israel and Hamas, with differences over who has the right to exploit it and who will benefit economically. These disputes further complicate the search for a peaceful solution to the conflict and can lead to greater tension and violence.

The lack of resources and their inequitable distribution have a direct impact on the living conditions of the Palestinian population, contributing to poverty, inequality and frustration. This, in turn, can fuel feelings of injustice and resentment toward Israel and support support for groups like Hamas, which promise to fight for the rights and well-being of the Palestinian people.

Effectively addressing issues related to natural and territorial resources requires an inclusive and multilateral approach that takes into account the concerns and interests of all parties involved. This may involve negotiating agreements on the shared management of water resources, the withdrawal of illegal settlements, and reaching an agreement on a two-state solution based on the 1967 borders with East Jerusalem as its shared capital.

However, the complexity and sensitivity of these issues make them difficult to resolve and require continued commitment and bold political leadership from all stakeholders. Only through constructive dialogue and genuine political will can we address the roots of the conflict and create the basis for lasting peace and shared prosperity in the region.

In the context of the conflict between Israel and Hamas, the role of natural and territorial resources is intrinsically linked to the issue of Israel's occupation and control of the Palestinian territories. This control also extends to natural resources, such as water and soil, which have become sources of tension and conflict.

Access to water is one of the main conflict issues in the region. Israel, through its military and administrative authority, has almost complete control of the West Bank's water resources, including underground aquifers and rivers. This control results in an unequal distribution of water resources, with Israelis having access to significantly more water than Palestinians. This disparity creates serious difficulties for Palestinians, who often face water shortages and restrictions in their access to drinking water.

In addition, the expansion of Israeli settlements in the West Bank and East Jerusalem is a source of constant tension. These settlements are considered illegal under international law and undermine the prospects for a two-state solution, since they reduce the space available for a future Palestinian state and create territorial divisions that make it difficult to establish a definitive border between Israel and Palestine.

The Gaza Strip, with its limited natural resources and extremely high population density, is also at the center of many disputes. The blockade imposed by Israel has limited the access of the population of

Gaza to essential resources such as food, water, energy and construction materials. This has led to serious economic and humanitarian difficulties, with devastating consequences for the civilian population.

At the same time, control of natural resources can be a source of power and control for both sides. For example, the natural gas field off the coast of Gaza has become an object of contention between Israel and Hamas, with both sides seeking to exploit this resource for their economic and political advantage.

In conclusion, natural and territorial resources play a crucial role in perpetuating the conflict between Israel and Hamas, fueling tensions and disputes over land, water and energy resources. Addressing these issues requires a serious commitment to a political and negotiated solution to the conflict, one that takes into account the concerns and interests of both sides and that promotes justice, dignity and security for everyone in the region.

In the context of the conflict between Israel and Hamas, the role of natural and territorial resources is crucial to understanding the complex dynamics that fuel tensions in the Middle East region. Natural resources, including water, land and natural gas, and land control are at the center of disputes between the two parties involved in the conflict.

Access to and control of water resources are a major source of conflict in the region. Water is a precious and indispensable resource for life and development, and the control of water sources has become a strategic objective for both parties. Israel controls most of the region's water resources, including underground aquifers and rivers, and this has created a disparity in access to water between Israelis and Palestinians. This imbalance in access to water has led to serious difficulties for

Palestinians, with chronic water shortages and limitations in the supply of water for domestic, agricultural and industrial purposes.

Control of territories is another central aspect of the conflict. Israel maintains a military occupation of the West Bank, including East Jerusalem, and has maintained a land, sea and air blockade on Gaza since 2007. This control of the Palestinian territories has led to continued human rights violations, demolitions of Palestinian homes, confiscation of land and construction of illegal Israeli settlements, all of which fuel tensions and hinder the prospect of a two-state solution.

In addition, the search for and exploitation of natural resources, such as natural gas off the coast of Gaza, have become the subject of dispute between Israel and Hamas. Gas reserves could represent a crucial source of economic wealth for the Gaza Strip, but the lack of an agreement between Israel and

Hamas on how to exploit these resources has led to continued tensions and hampered the region's economic development.

Overall, control of natural and territorial resources is a key factor in perpetuating the conflict between Israel and Hamas, fueling tensions, undermining trust and hampering progress toward a peaceful and sustainable solution to the conflict. Addressing these issues requires a serious commitment to justice, fairness and dignity for both parties involved, as well as a constructive and negotiated dialogue that takes into account the concerns and interests of all stakeholders.

The natural and territorial resources in the conflict between Israel and Hamas represent an intricate knot of tensions and conflicts that profoundly influence the dynamics of the Middle East region.

The control of water resources is a major source of controversy. In an already arid region, water has become a precious and scarce resource, and its control has become a matter of national security. Israel, with its military and technological superiority, has almost complete control of water resources, including aquifers in the West Bank. This control translates into disparity in access to water between Israelis and Palestinians, with serious consequences for the Palestinian population, who often suffer from water shortages and restrictions on access to drinking water.

Control of territories is another crucial aspect of the conflict. Israel maintains a military occupation of the West Bank and has isolated the Gaza Strip with a land, sea and air blockade. This territorial control greatly limits the freedom of movement of Palestinians, affecting every aspect of their daily lives, from access to health services to education and work. In addition, the expansion of Israeli settlements into occupied Palestinian territory is considered illegal under international law and undermines the prospect of a two-state solution, creating tensions and causing violence on the ground.

Natural resources such as natural gas off the coast of Gaza are another point of contention. While gas reserves could provide a crucial source of economic wealth for the people of Gaza, disputes over exploitation and revenue distribution have hampered any significant progress toward sustainable exploitation of these resources.

Globally, control of natural and territorial resources fuels tensions, undermines peace efforts, and perpetuates the cycle of violence and suffering in the Middle East region. Effectively addressing these issues requires a determined commitment to a negotiated political solution that respects the rights of both parties and promotes justice and dignity for everyone in the region.

In conclusion, the control of natural and territorial resources is a central element in the conflict between Israel and Hamas, with significant implications for the daily lives of the peoples involved and for the prospects for peace in the Middle East region. Addressing these issues requires a genuine commitment to dialogue and negotiation, together with a mutual recognition of the rights and concerns of both parties. Only through an inclusive process that respects the principles of justice and human dignity can we hope to end the conflict and build a future of peace and prosperity for everyone in the region.

21. Personal reflections on humanity and tolerance in situations of conflict.

Personal reflections on humanity and tolerance in situations of conflict are profound and complex, as we are faced with the challenge of maintaining our compassion and understanding even in the most difficult circumstances.
First, it's important to recognize that conflict doesn't make individuals less human. Even when the actions of the fighters may seem inhuman, it is essential to remember that behind every action there are people with feelings, hopes and suffering. Maintaining this human perspective can be difficult, but it's critical

to maintaining a sense of empathy and compassion, even toward those with whom we disagree.

Tolerance, in particular, becomes crucial in times of conflict. It implies respect and acceptance of differences, despite political, religious or cultural differences. In conflict situations, tolerance can be tested as people tend to adhere to their convictions more fervently. However, it is precisely in these moments that tolerance becomes more important than ever, since it can promote dialogue, mutual understanding and, in the end, peace.

A fundamental aspect of personal reflection is also self-awareness. It is important to question our opinions, prejudices and privileges, and to understand how these may influence our perceptions of the conflict and those involved. Being aware of our limitations and our partialities allows us to be more open to dialogue and to building bridges, rather than walls, between people.

Finally, conflict situations can provide opportunities for personal growth and transformation. Through challenge and difficulty, we can learn to develop greater resilience, compassion, and understanding. These experiences can lead us to reflect on our values and priorities in life, prompting us to seek more constructive ways to address differences and resolve conflicts.

Ultimately, personal reflections on humanity and tolerance in situations of conflict invite us to recognize our common humanity, to embrace diversity and to commit to a peace based on mutual understanding and respect for fundamental human rights. Only through a collective commitment to tolerance and compassion can we hope to build a more just, equitable and peaceful world for all.

In situations of conflict, personal reflections on humanity and tolerance can lead to deep introspection and a richer understanding of the complexities of the human being.

One of the first challenges is to maintain one's humanity and compassion even in the face of the most violent and inhuman actions. It's easy to get overwhelmed by negative emotions generated by conflict, such as anger, fear, or resentment. However, it is precisely in these moments that it is essential to remember our common humanity and try to understand the motivations and suffering of others, even if they may seem so different from us.

Tolerance therefore becomes an objective to be pursued with even greater determination. Tolerance does not necessarily mean accepting the actions or opinions of others, but rather respecting them as individuals and recognizing their right to human dignity and freedom of expression. In a context of conflict, tolerance can be a bridge to mutual understanding and constructive dialogue, fundamental elements for the search for peaceful and lasting solutions.

Conflict situations can also test our ability to look beyond differences and to find points of contact with others. This can require a great deal of empathy and understanding, especially when opinions and experiences are so different from ours. However, it is precisely through these efforts that we can overcome divisions and build meaningful connections that can help reduce tensions and promote peace. Finally, personal reflections on conflict can push us to consider our role and responsibility in confronting injustices and promoting positive change. Even though we may feel powerless in the face of the vastness of conflict-related issues, every small action counts. We can seek to educate others, to spread messages of peace, and to promote tolerance in our community and beyond.

Ultimately, personal reflections on humanity and tolerance in situations of conflict invite us to explore our capacity for empathy, compassion and understanding for others. Through an ongoing commitment to maintaining our humanity and promoting tolerance, we can help create a more just, inclusive and peaceful world for all.

In contexts of conflict, reflections on human nature and tolerance become even more relevant and complex. Conflict itself tests our values and our ability to treat others with compassion and respect, but it can also provide opportunities for personal growth and transformation.

One of the most significant challenges is to maintain an intact humanity despite adverse circumstances. Conflict often brings with it violence, suffering, and loss, which can erode our sensitivity and compassion. However, it is precisely at these critical moments that we must reaffirm our fundamental human values and recognize the dignity and intrinsic value of every human being, regardless of their role in the conflict.

Tolerance becomes crucial in a context of conflict, since respect and acceptance of differences can help reduce tensions and promote peaceful coexistence.

However, tolerance doesn't necessarily mean being indifferent or passively accepting injustices. On the contrary, it may mean recognizing the legitimate aspirations and rights of all groups involved in the conflict, even as we strive to find constructive ways to resolve differences.

Personal reflections on the conflict can also lead to a deeper exploration of our identity and privileges. We can question ourselves how our positions, our experiences and our social context influence our perceptions of the conflict and of the people involved.

This self-reflection may be uncomfortable, but it is essential to develop a greater awareness of our partialities and to engage in a more empathetic and inclusive dialogue.

Finally, conflict situations can provide opportunities for personal growth and transformation. Through challenge and difficulty, we can learn to develop greater resilience, compassion, and understanding. These experiences can lead us to reconsider our values and priorities in life, prompting us to seek more constructive ways to address differences and resolve conflicts.

In conclusion, personal reflections on humanity and tolerance in situations of conflict invite us to reaffirm our fundamental values of human dignity, compassion and mutual respect. They are a reminder of our ability to grow through challenges and to commit to a more just, inclusive and peaceful world for all.

Ultimately, personal reflections on humanity and tolerance in situations of conflict push us to a profound exploration of the fundamental values that define us as human beings. They are a constant reminder of our ability to maintain compassion and empathy even in the most difficult circumstances, recognizing the intrinsic dignity of every individual involved in the conflict. These reflections also invite us to recognize our role and responsibility in promoting tolerance and mutual understanding, thus contributing to the construction of a more just, inclusive and peaceful world for all. Through an ongoing commitment to cultivate our humanity and promote tolerance, we can hope to transform conflicts into opportunities for growth and positive change, paving the way for lasting and meaningful peace.

In conclusion, the book thoroughly examined the conflict between Israel and

Hamas, exploring its historical roots, immediate causes, military strategies, effects on the civilian population, and regional and international implications. We have analyzed the role of natural and territorial resources in perpetuating conflict, in addition to personal reflections on humanity and tolerance in conflict situations.

For those who wish to further deepen their understanding of the Israeli-Palestinian conflict, there are numerous resources available online. Websites such as the Middle East Monitor (https://www.middleeastmonitor.com/) and Al Jazeera (https://www.aljazeera.com/) offer in-depth news coverage and analysis of the latest news and developments in the region. In addition, organizations such as Amnesty International (https://www.amnesty.org/) and Human Rights Watch (https://www.hrw.org/)

provide detailed reports on human rights violations in the context of the conflict.

For those interested in a larger historical perspective, it is advisable to consult resources such as the Council on Foreign Relations website (https://www.cfr.org/), which provides in-depth analyses of the history and politics of the conflict, along with interactive maps and other educational tools.

Finally, for those who wish to learn more about peace initiatives and attempts to resolve the conflict, we recommend consulting organizations such as Peace Now (https://peacenow.org.il/en) and the International Crisis Group (https://www.crisisgroup.org/), which work to promote peace and stability in the region through diplomacy and dialogue.

We hope that this book has provided a comprehensive overview of the Israeli-Palestinian conflict and has stimulated reflection and understanding of the complexity of the issues involved.

www.ingramcontent.com/pod-product-compliance
Lightning Source LLC
Chambersburg PA
CBHW050328160726
48002CB00001B/232